Complete Close Reading

BOOK 1

Jenny Thomas
Kirsten Owens

Australia • Brazil • Japan • Korea • Mexico • Singapore • Spain • United Kingdom • United States

Complete Close Reading Book one
1st Edition
Jenny Thomas
Kirsten Owens

Text design: Melissa Middleton
Cover design: Brenda Cantell

Any URLs contained in this publication were checked for currency during the production process. Note, however, that the publisher cannot vouch for the ongoing currency of URLs.

Acknowledgements
The authors and publisher gratefully credit or acknowledge permission to reproduce extracts from the following sources:
ACP Publishing, 'The True You', Dolly magazine, December 2002, ACP Publishing: Sydney, 2002. Reproduced by courtesy of Dolly magazine; Allen & Unwin, Cartoon 'Sheilas' from Real Gorgeous by Kaz Cooke, Allen & Unwin: St Leonards, 1994, map and text from Lionheart: A Journey of the Human Spirit by Jesse Martin with Ed Gannon (ed.), Allen & Unwin: St Leonards, 2000; Christopher Little Literary Agency on behalf of JK Rowling, Harry Potter and the Philosopher's Stone by JK Rowling, Bloomsbury Publishing: London, 1997. Copyright © JK Rowling 1997; Filmlnk magazine, Rabbit Proof Fence and 'Phillip Noyce: Rabbit Proof Fence Director' by Erin Free, Filmlnk magazine, www.filmink.com.au; Gareth Stevens Inc., Reprinted with permission from the Acid Rain Hazard by Judith Woodburn. Copyright © 1992 by Gareth Stevens, Inc. All rights reserved; Harcourt Inc., Counting Crocodiles by Judy Sierra from The Age Summer Book Guide, The Age: Melbourne, November 2001; Hodder & Stoughton Ltd, The World of the Medieval Knight by Christopher Gravett, Hodder Children's Books: London, 1993. Reproduced by permission of Hodder & Stoughton Limited; Oxford University Press Australia, reproduced by permission of Oxford University Press Australia from The Australian Pocket Oxford Dictionary by Bruce Moore (ed.) © 1996 Oxford University Press, www.oup.com.au and The Australian Student's Thesaurus by Anne Knight (ed.) © 1991 Oxford University Press, www.oup.com.au; Pan Macmillan, Rocketship Gallileo by R Heinlein from Classic Science Fiction by Peter Haining (ed.), Macmillan: London, 1995; Pearson Education Australia, The World of Science, Book 2, 2nd edn by David Heffernan and Mark Learmonth, Longman Cheshire: Melbourne, 1992; Kathleen Priest, 'My Dad' by Kathleen Priest from Nothing Interesting about Cross Street edited by Beth Yahp, Angus & Robertson: Sydney 1996; University of Queensland Press, Crossfire by James Moloney, University of Queensland Press: St Lucia, 1992 and A Bridge to Wiseman's Cove by James Moloney, University of Queensland Press: St Lucia, 1996; Thursday Plantation Labaratories Ltd, advertisement 'Natural Acne Treatment'; JET magazine, March 2006 for Bang On, www.jetmag.co.nz; Jack Davis, Death of a Tree in John and Dorothy Colmere Through Auustralian Eyes: Prose and Poetry for Schools, Macmillan 1984.

Every attempt has been made to trace and acknowledge copyright holders. Where the attempt has been unsuccessful, the publisher welcomes information that would redress the situation.

For product information and technology assistance,
in Australia call **1300 790 853**;
in New Zealand call **0800 449 725**

For permission to use material from this text or product, please email **aust.permissions@cengage.com**

National Library of New Zealand Cataloguing-in-Publication Data
Thomas, Jenny
Complete Close Reading. Book one / Jenny Thomas, Kirsten Owens.
ISBN 978 0 17 013306 7
1. Reading comprehension–Problems, exercises, etc. I. Owens, Kirsten. II Title.
428.43076–dc 22

Cengage Learning Australia
Level 7, 80 Dorcas Street
South Melbourne, Victoria Australia 3205

Cengage Learning New Zealand
Unit 4B Rosedale Office Park
331 Rosedale Road, Albany, North Shore 0632, NZ

For learning solutions, visit **cengage.com.au**

Printed in China by 1010 Printing International Limited.
17 18 19 20 21 22 23 25 24 23 22 21

Contents

Introduction

DEAR COLLEAGUE

As teachers of English we know that a student's ability to effectively and efficiently read, understand, analyse, interpret and respond to text is a significant focus in the senior English classroom. Therefore we appreciate the need to begin teaching students the basic skills required to effectively read and understand a text in our junior classes. *Complete Close Reading* provides a consistent approach to developing and practising the vitally important skills of reading with comprehension and/or responding to written, visual and oral texts.

Although the focus of many current assessments is strongly geared towards the achieved, merit, excellence system, *Complete Close Reading* holds to the idea that you can't run before you walk and, therefore, divides its questions into sections that bring together the best ideas from standards-based assessment, three level reading guides and the tried and tested straightforward comprehension questions approach to give you a textbook that focuses on developing those essential skills rather than the final summative assessment. It would be expected that you as a teacher (and school examinations) would reflect an individual school's assessment and reporting methods.

Each unit is organised into five sections:

On the surface

These are basic literal questions. Students should be able to find the answer clearly written in the text.

Discovering techniques

These are questions about the purpose, structure and features of the text. Students will need to focus on the intended audience, the language used and the way the text has been constructed.

Search and think

These are inferential or interpretive questions. Students will have to use their own knowledge and thinking, as well as information from the text, to answer questions in this section.

Hidden depths

These are creative, critical or high-order-thinking questions. Students will need to respond to this section as individuals and be prepared to justify their responses.

Extend yourself

These are more open-ended questions. They provide a range of opportunities for students to respond to the text at a deeper level by writing, viewing, listening and speaking. As the title of the section suggests, these would be most useful as extension, homework, extended absences or last period on a Friday afternoon.

In addition *Complete Close Reading* provides a system of ongoing assessment so that individual improvement can be recorded and monitored over time by both the students and their teacher. Following each unit, students should record their progress on a Student Assessment Record Sheet, while teachers are encouraged to keep records of individual and group progress using the Assessment Record Sheet. Blackline masters for both sheets are printed on pages 75-77 of the *Complete Close Reading Teacher Answer Book*.

Complete Close Reading provides good models of a wide range of text types, incorporating many areas of secondary school study.

Complete Close Reading acknowledges the importance of difference and diversity in both the texts selected and in the opportunity for teachers and students to tailor the use of each unit to cater for individual differences in ability, language background and learning style. Teachers are encouraged to assist students to decide which questions are most appropriate for their ability, preferred learning styles and the time available. *Complete Close Reading* can be used in class for individual, group or whole class work and at home for homework and revision.

We hope you enjoy using the variety of texts explored in *Complete Close Reading* and assisting students to take literacy into many areas of school and life.

JENNY THOMAS AND KIRSTEN OWENS

Helpful hints

The following pre-reading strategies are recommended for students before attempting each unit:

1 **FOCUS** on the text type and title.

2 **THINK** about where and why these text types are used.

3 **RECALL** any prior experience with this type of text or this topic.

4 **PREDICT** what the text may be about and how it is likely to be structured.

5 **READ** the text carefully.

6 **SCAN** the text for difficult or unfamiliar words or phrases. Work out the meanings for this vocabulary by using the context of the passage, consulting a dictionary or discussing the words with the teacher or peers.

7 **READ** the text again. The following strategies may assist students while they read each text .
- Ask questions about the text and answer them while reading.
- Visualise what is happening in the text.
- Summarise the text in dot points.
- Explain the text to a peer.

Remember, this is not a race.

8 **WORK** through the questions one at a time. Remember two important skills:

1 **Scanning:** Where instead of reading word for word, your eyes are searching quickly through something looking for a specific thing. Some people use a finger or a ruler to help them scan.

2 **Skimming:** Most commonly used to 'skim read' a written text to locate relevant information. Start by:

a identifying the key words (scanning) in the questions, which will show you where the answers are in the text;

b skim reading the text by sliding your eyes down the middle of the page or moving your finger across the page looking for key words;

c and when you find the key word, quickly read around it to find the answer to the question.

UNIT 1 The Deputy Principal

TEXT TYPE Narrative
PURPOSE To tell a story
STRUCTURE 1 Orientation – who or what, where or when
2 Complication
3 Series of events
4 Resolution
FEATURES Use of past tense and pronouns

From *Crossfire* by James Moloney

The Deputy Principal scurried along the corridor, his leather shoes pounding the old wooden floorboards like hammers. Two unhappy boys, heads down and shoulders hunched, hurried to stay in his wake. As the little procession passed each classroom, heads were lowered again, like animals in a field returning to their quiet grazing. When they reached the bank of grey metal lockers, the marchers halted and the Deputy Principal said simply, 'Aldridge, I want you to get out your guitar case.'

Luke Aldridge stepped forward. Though only fourteen, he was almost as tall as the Deputy Principal, but whereas the Deputy was a ball of a man, with muscular arms and legs and a head that seemed to sit on his shoulders without need of a neck, Luke was slim and angular. His movements were awkward; he hadn't yet learned to control his rapidly growing body. And now he was nervous, which made his movements even more clumsy as he worked the dial of the combination lock. It fell open, and as instructed he withdrew a black guitar case, ancient and battered, made from the rigid cardboard used before vinyl and plastic became available. It was secured by two catches speckled with rust.

'Open it,' commanded the Deputy Principal.

'It's locked and I don't have the key,' Luke said.

'Don't give me that! This is your case isn't it?'

But the Deputy was deprived his full measure of anger when the second boy interrupted, digging into his pocket.

'I have the key, Sir.'

'Is that so? Interesting. Well then, you open it, Tertzowjic.' He pronounced the name perfectly and couldn't resist a satisfied smile to himself at the evident surprise this confident performance produced. Most who confronted this name baulked and stammered their way through it.

The second boy, who now held the tiny key in his hand, took the guitar case from his companion and placed it carefully on the floor. Kneeling beside it, he inserted the key in each lock in turn, then released both spring-loaded latches together, with a 'flick-thud' sound. The boy hesitated then, head bowed, and a second later the Deputy Principal denied him the dubious honour of raising the lid. Instead, he hooked the toe of his shoe under the rim and flipped it upwards.

All three stood gazing at the contents without the least surprise. After all, why should there be any surprise? The two boys had both known exactly what was inside and the Deputy Principal had certainly expected to see what lay before him now. That was why this little melodrama was being played out.

On the surface [Literal comprehension – right-there questions]

1. Who is in trouble with the Deputy Principal?
2. In whose locker is the guitar case?
3. Why can't Luke open the guitar case?
4. What is the guitar case made out of?
5. Why weren't any of them surprised at what was in the case?

Optional assessment: 5 x 1 mark = 5 marks

Discovering techniques [Language structures and features, spelling, grammar, vocabulary]

1. Look up the following words in a dictionary and write out their meanings. Remember to keep in context with the passage.
   a principal b principle c scurried d hunched
   e baulked f dubious g melodrama
2. Similes are comparisons that use the word 'like' or 'as', e.g. It was light as day.
   Give two examples of similes from this extract.
3. Outline the sequence of events in the Deputy Principal's melodrama.
4. Would this melodrama have been as effective if the Deputy Principal had told the boys what he knew before he marched them down to their lockers? Why?/Why not?

Optional assessment: 4 x 2 marks = 8 marks

Search and think [Inferential and interpretive comprehension]

1. What do the students in the classrooms do when the procession passes their room?
2. Thinking about how the characters are described in the passage, who do you think the writer's sympathy lies with: the boys or the Deputy Principal? Explain your choice.
3. Can we assume that the guitar case belongs to Aldridge? Explain your answer.
4. How do we know the boys are worried about what the Deputy Principal is about to find in the case?
5. Why do you think the Deputy Principal opens the case with his foot?

Optional assessment: 5 x 1 mark = 5 marks

Hidden depths [Creative comprehension – responding personally, higher-order-thinking skills, making links]

1. The guitar case obviously does not contain a guitar. What do you think is in the case?
2. The Deputy Principal seems to be pleased that he has caught the boys. What do you think his attitude is to the boys?

Optional assessment: 2 x 2 marks = 4 marks

Extend yourself [Links to real life or other literature, researching, writing, creating, speaking tasks]

- Script the conversation between the Deputy Principal and the person who informed on the boys.
- Write the next scene in the story. What was in the guitar case?
- Sketch the scene based on the descriptions in this text.
- Present a role play of this passage to the class.
- Write your own story about students being caught doing something wrong. Try to capture the behaviour of the students and the attitude of the teacher by using dialogue and descriptive language. Try including some similes.
- Write your own account of being caught. Try to capture the sights, sounds and thoughts you experienced.

UNIT 2 To Castle Dracula

TEXT TYPE	Journal or diary
PURPOSE	To reconstruct past experiences by retelling events in the order in which they have occurred
STRUCTURE	1 Orientation – background information about who, where and when 2 Series of events in chronological order 3 A personal comment
FEATURES	Abbreviations, informal language, varied sentences, personal reflections

Jonathan Harker's Journal from Bram Stoker's Dracula

3 May. Bistritz. - Left Munich at 8.35 p.m., on 1st May, arriving at Vienna early next morning; should have arrived at 6.46, but train was an hour late. Buda-Pesth seems a wonderful place, from the glimpse which I got of it from the train and the little I could walk through the streets. I feared to go very far from the station, as we had arrived late and would start as near the correct time as possible. The impression I had was that we were leaving the West and entering the East; the most Western of splendid bridges over the Danube, which is here of noble width and depth, took us among the traditions of Turkish rule.

We left in pretty good time, and came after nightfall to Klausenburgh. Here I stopped for the night at the Hotel Royale. I had for dinner, or rather supper, a chicken done up some way with red pepper, which was good but thirsty. (Mem., get recipe for Mina.) I asked the waiter, and he said it was called 'paprika hendl,' and that, as it was a national dish, I should be able to get it anywhere along the Carpathians. I found my smattering of German very useful here; indeed, I don't know how I should be able to get on without it.

Having some time at my disposal when in London, I had visited the British Museum, and made search among the books and maps in the library regarding Transylvania; it had struck me that some foreknowledge of the country could hardly fail to have some importance in dealing with a noble of that country. I find that the district he named is in the extreme east of the country, just on the borders of three states, Transylvania, Moldavia, and Bukovina, in the midst of the Carpathian mountains; one of the wildest and least known portions of Europe. I was not able to light on any map or work giving the exact locality of the Castle Dracula, as there are no maps of this country as yet to compare with our own Ordnance Survey maps; but I found that Bistritz, the post town named by Count Dracula, is a fairly well-known place.

On the surface [Literal comprehension – right-there questions]

1 Between which cities did Jonathan Harker travel?
2 At what time and on what date did Jonathan leave Munich?
3 What form or mode of transport was Jonathan using?
4 What are the main ingredients of 'paprika hendl'?
5 What does Jonathan note to himself as a reminder?
   a To get 'paprika hendl' in Carpathians
   b To get a recipe for Mina
   c To get a map showing Castle Dracula

Optional assessment: 5 x 1 mark = 5 marks

Discovering techniques [Language structures and features, spelling, grammar, vocabulary]

1 Using a theasarus find synonyms (words with the same or similar meanings) for the following phrases as they are used in this text.

a glimpse	b impression	c splendid	d nightfall
e thirsty	f time at my disposal	g smattering	h extreme

Optional assessment: 1 x 2 marks = 2 marks

Search and think [Inferential and interpretive comprehension]

1 Jonathan is able to speak at least two languages. What are they?
2 Why is Jonathan travelling to Bistritz?
   a For a holiday
   b To experience different cultures
   c To meet Count Dracula
3 How has Jonathan tried to prepare for his journey and meeting?
4 Where and what are the Carpathians? (Hint: You may need to refer to an atlas.)
5 List clues which indicate that this diary is not set in modern times.

Optional assessment: 5 x 2 marks = 10 marks

Hidden depths [Creative comprehension – responding personally, higher-order-thinking skills, making links]

1 Who do you think Mina could be? Give reasons.
2 How do you think Jonathan Harker was feeling during this journey? Justify your answer.

Optional assessment: 2 x 3 marks = 6 marks

Extend yourself [Links to real life or other literature, researching, writing, creating, speaking tasks]

- Investigate the history and legend of Dracula and write a short report.
- Use the entertainment guide in a newspaper to research the types or genres of films currently being shown at cinemas. What proportion of current films could be classified as horror or thrillers?
- Investigate why readers and viewers enjoy the horror genre. Write a dot-point summary of your findings.

UNIT 3

School camp

TEXT TYPE Recount
PURPOSE To reconstruct past experiences by retelling events in the order in which they have occurred
STRUCTURE
1 Orientation – background information about who, where and when
2 Series of events in chronological order
3 A personal comment (optional)
FEATURES Uses past tense, action verbs, descriptive language, may include quotes

Camp Scorcher

We set off for Camp Scorcher on Monday morning. We were due to leave at 9 a.m. but it took ages to pack all the gear into the bus so we were 20 minutes late.

We arrived at Camp Scorcher at about 2 p.m. and were shown where our huts were. I was in Hut 4.

After we unpacked we had 'orientation' – lots of talk and rules. Then we had free time, dinner (roast lamb), and a night walk. It was fun but a bit scary walking in the bush at night. We saw a wallaby and a few possums and millions of trees.

Tuesday was a scorcher – so hot the road started to melt and get sticky! We did activities from a roster. It was our turn for archery, raft building and low ropes. Our raft collapsed! At night we had a BBQ and told stories around the campfire.

On Wednesday we did high ropes, canoeing and flying fox. We swam most of the afternoon because it was still scorching. Dinner was chicken and salad. After dinner we worked on our comedy skit for 'Red Faces Night'.

Thursday we did the challenge course. Our hut came 2nd by 17 seconds. We made up for it by winning 'Red Faces' though. Our skit was hilarious. Dinner was Spag. Bol.

On Friday we had to clean up the huts, pack up our gear and have a presentation of awards. I got a certificate of participation and a chocolate bar for being in the winning hut for 'Red Faces'.

The bus trip home was long and boring. We were all tired and a bit sad to be going back to normal life after such a great week together.

Camp Scorcher was fun and it certainly lived up to its name.

On the surface [Literal comprehension – right-there questions]

1 Which camp did the student attend?
2 How long was the student at the camp?
3 What type of vehicle was used to transport the students to camp?
4 What main meals were served at camp?
5 List the activities available to students at this camp.

Optional assessment: 5 x 1 mark = 5 marks

Discovering techniques [Language structures and features, spelling, grammar, vocabulary]

1 Look up the following words in a dictionary and write out their meanings.
   a scorcher b skit
2 List examples of informal language (everyday, colloquial or personal language) and abbreviation used in this text.
3 List examples of exaggerated language or hyperbole in this text (e.g. 'hilarious').
4 Using the information in this text, copy and complete the following table.

Day	Activities	Main meal
Monday	Orientation, night walk	
↓		
Friday		

Optional assessment: 5 x 2 marks = 10 marks

Search and think [Inferential and interpretive comprehension]

1 Which activities do you think the student enjoyed most at camp? Why?
2 What do you think the student meant by 'it certainly lived up to its name'?
3 Why did the students have to participate in 'Red Faces'?
4 Do you think this student is competitive? Give evidence.
5 Why do you think the students were feeling tired and sad on their way back to school at the end of the camp?

Optional assessment: 5 x 2 marks = 10 marks

Hidden depths [Creative comprehension – responding personally, higher-order-thinking skills, making links]

1 What do students learn by going on camp?
   a Independence b Cooperation c Tolerance
   d How to tackle challenges e All of the above
2 This student had a 'great week'. How do you think a shy, studious student would have felt about this camp experience and why?

Optional assessment: 2 x 2 marks = 4 marks

Extend yourself [Links to real life or other literature, researching, writing, creating, speaking tasks]

- Draw an imaginary map of Camp Scorcher. Show the location of buildings and activities.
- Camp Scorcher is focused on physical challenges and does not cater for shy, artistic, disabled or vegetarian students. With a partner, discuss whether or not this is a problem. Create a more inclusive and varied programme of activities and meals for Camp Everybody.

UNIT 4 Job hunting

TEXT TYPE Business letter
PURPOSE To apply for a position
STRUCTURE
1 Name (if known), title, address
2 Date
3 Formal greeting
4 Response to criteria
5 Sign off
FEATURES Set layout, formal language

I wish to apply for the position

J. Clark
12a Knights Rd
Rothesay Bay

17 March 2007

Human Resources Manager
The Warehouse
Glenfield

Dear Sir,

I wish to apply for the position of Casual Sales Assistant at The Warehouse (Glenfield) advertised in the North Shore Times on 15 March 2007.

I am a 15-year-old high school student studying Year 11 at Westlake Boys' High School. I am keen to gain experience in the retail sector. I received very good results for English, Mathematics, History and French.

My interests include sport and reading. I am the captain of the school basketball team as well as being a keen cricketer. These sports have allowed me to develop my skills as a team player. I am a reliable and punctual person and I would enjoy the opportunity to learn about the workforce.

Please find enclosed my curriculum vitae and a reference. I am available for an interview at your convenience.

Yours faithfully

Jasper Clark

Jasper Clark

On the surface [Literal comprehension – right-there questions]

1 How old is the applicant?
2 What is the job being applied for?
3 What is a reference?
4 Why does the applicant mention he is reliable and punctual?
5 Give each paragraph a title which indicates its contents.

Optional assessment: 5 x 1 mark = 5 marks

Discovering techniques [Language structures and features, spelling, grammar, vocabulary]

1 Simple sentences are sentences that contain one main idea. Copy the simple sentences from the list below.
   a My interests include sport and reading.
   b I am a reliable and punctual person and I would enjoy the opportunity to learn about the workforce.
   c I am a 15-year-old high-school student studying Year 11 at Westlake Boys' High School.
   d I received very good results for English, Mathematics, History and French.
2 Business letters have a formal tone. Just as we give spoken language a tone, such as angry, we can give writing a tone by selecting particular words and sentence structures.
   How is a formal tone created in the letter?

Optional assessment: 2 x 2 marks = 4 marks

Search and think [Inferential and interpretive comprehension]

1 What kind of person is the applicant?
2 What kind of requirements do you think were specified in the job advertisement?
3 What is a curriculum vitae and how does this differ from a letter of application?
4 What aspects of Jasper's academic work would be most relevant to the position?
5 Do you think the applicant's sporting interests are of relevance to the job? Why?/Why not?

Optional assessment: 5 x 1 mark = 5 marks

Hidden depths [Creative comprehension – responding personally, higher-order-thinking skills, making links]

1 What research would you recommend the applicant complete before attending a job interview?
2 This job was advertised in the newspaper. List at least two other ways of finding out about jobs.
3 What are the benefits of teenagers having part-time jobs?

Optional assessment: 3 x 2 marks = 6 marks

Extend yourself [Links to real life or other literature, researching, writing, creating, speaking tasks]

- Research how to write a CV (curriculum vitae) and put together one for yourself.
- Find two job advertisements from different fields. Write a letter in response to each of these advertisements, taking care to adjust your style according to the job.
- Write an advertisement for your 'dream' job.
- Write a list of guidelines advising students on how to find part-time work.

UNIT 5 'Prisoner' to 'prize'

TEXT TYPE	Dictionary
PURPOSE	To give the meaning, pronunciation, grammatical use and history of words in a language
STRUCTURE	1 Head word; 2 Pronunciation; 3 Part of speech; 4 Definitions; 5 Phrases these words are used in; 6 Derivations; 7 Cross-references; 8 Etymology (origin)
FEATURES	Abbreviations, font changes

From *The Pocket Oxford Dictionary*

prisoner of conscience **prize**[1]

prisoner of conscience see CONSCIENCE.

privacy /pruy-vuh-see, priv-uh-/ *n.* **1 a** state of being private and undisturbed. **b** person's right to this. **2** freedom from intrusion or public attention. **3** avoidance of publicity.

private /pruy-vuht/ — *adj.* **1** belonging to an individual, one's own, personal (private property). **2** confidential, not to be disclosed to others (private talks). **3** kept or removed from public knowledge or observation. **4** not open to the public (a private road). **5** (of a place) secluded; affording privacy. **6** (of a person) not holding public office or an official position. **7** (of education or medical treatment) conducted outside the publicly funded system, at the individual's expense. — *n.* **1** private soldier. **2** (in pl.) *colloq.* genitals. □ **in private** privately. □ **privately** adv. [Latin privo privat- deprive]

private eye *n. colloq.* private investigator.

privatise /pruy-vuh-tuyz/ v. (also **-ize**) (-sing or -zing) transfer (a business etc.) from government to private ownership.
□ **privatisation** /-zay-shuhn/ *n.*

privet / priv-uht/ *n.* bushy evergreen European shrub used for hedges. [origin unknown]

privilege /priv-uh-lij/ — *n.* **1** a right, advantage, or immunity, belonging to a person, class, or office. **b** (in full **parliamentary privilege**) special right of members of parliament to speak freely in parliament without the risk of prosecution they might incur if they said the same things outside. **2** Law the right of a lawyer, priest or minister of religion, doctor, etc., to refuse to disclose communications made by a client, penitent, patient, etc., in the course of a professional relationship. **3** special benefit or honour (a privilege to meet you). – *v.* (**-ging**) **1** invest with a privilege. **2** (foll. by to + infin.) allow (a person) as a privilege (to do something). 3 (often foll. by from) exempt (a person from a liability etc.). □ **privileged** *adj.* [Latin: related to PRIVY, lex leg- law]

privy /priv-ee/ — *adj.* **1** (foll. by to) sharing in the secret of (a person's plans etc.) (too many were privy to his plot for it to succeed). **2** archaic hidden, secret. — *n.* (*pl.* – **ies**) toilet, esp. an outside one. [French privé private place]

prize[1] — *n.* **1** something that can be won in a competition, lottery, etc. **2** reward given as a symbol of victory or superiority. **3** something striven for or worth striving for. **4** (attrib.) to which a prize is awarded (prize poem).

The Pocket Oxford Dictionary, 2nd edn, Oxford University Press

On the surface [Literal comprehension – right-there questions]

1 a How many definitions are there for the adjective 'private'?
  b How many definitions are there for the noun 'private'?
2 What word has a cross-reference as part of its definition?
3 What is the definition given for the noun 'private eye'?
4 What is written on the top left-hand side of the page?
5 What is the etymology of the word 'privately'?
6 The definitions are ranked. Which word has the most definitions?

Optional assessment: 6 x 1 mark = 6 marks

Discovering techniques [Language structures and features, spelling, grammar, vocabulary]

1 Dictionaries use many addreviations. Why do you think this is?
2 Write the following abbreviations out in full: *n.* *adj.* *coloq.* *adv.* *v.* *pl.*
3 Choose three words or phrases from the page and place them in a sentence that makes their meaning clear, e.g. private sector, privation, privatise.

Optional assessment: 3 x 2 marks = 6 marks

Search and think [Inferential and interpretive comprehension]

1 Why do dictionaries give the pronounciation of words?
2 What are 'privies'?
3 List some jobs where people have immunity to disclosure of information.
4 Which word is used to describe when a business is transferred (sold) from government ownership to private ownership?
5 Find the name of the shrub that is a serious pest in the New Zealand bush.
6 Find the word that describes both the state of being undisturbed and the right to being undisturbed.

Optional assessment: 6 x 1 mark = 6 marks

Hidden depths [Creative comprehension – responding personally, higher-order thinking skills, making links]

1 Write a set of instructions for efficient use of a dictionary. Think carefully about the steps and remember to explain clearly.
2 This extract deals with various types of privacy. Write about what privacy means to you.

Optional assessment: 2 x 2 marks = 4 marks

Extend yourself [Links to real life or other literature, researching, writing, creating, speaking tasks]

- Locate the dictionaries section in the library and list the different dictionaries you find there.
- Write an opinion piece on why doctors, lawyers, and ministers have immunity from disclosing information.

UNIT 6 Star cross'd lovers

TEXT TYPE Script
PURPOSE To entertain
STRUCTURE
1 Orientation – who or what, where and when
2 Complication
3 Series of events
4 Resolution

FEATURES Direct speech, stage directions

From *Romeo and Juliet*
by William Shakespeare

The prologue

[Enter CHORUS]

Two households, both alike in dignity,
In fair Verona, where we lay our scene,
From ancient grudge break to new mutiny,
Where civil blood makes civil hands unclean.
From forth the fatal loins of these two foes
A pair of star-cross'd lovers take their life;
Whose misadventur'd piteous overthrows
Doth with their death bury their parents' strife.
The fearful passage of their death-mark'd love,
And the continuance of their parents' rage,
Which, but their children's end, nought could remove,
Is now the two hours' traffic of our stage;
The which if you with patient ears attend,
What here shall miss, our toil shall strive to mend.
[Exit.]

On the surface [Literal comprehension – right-there questions]

1 Where is the play set?
2 What happens to the lovers?
3 What is a prologue?
4 What happened to the feud after the lovers died?
5 What is a modern word for 'foe'?

Optional assessment: 5 x 1 mark = 5 marks

Discovering techniques [Language structures and features, spelling, grammar, vocabulary]

1 An *iamb* is a metrical foot and is an unstressed syllable followed by a stressed syllable. Iambic pentameter is a five-foot line. That is, it consists of ten syllables and every second syllable is stressed. Count the syllables in each line of the prologue. Are there ten? Is every second syllable stressed?
2 Underline the stressed syllables in the following lines.
   a Two households both alike in dignity
   b In fair Verona where we lay our scene
   c From ancient grudge break to new mutiny

Optional assessment: 2 x 3 marks = 6 marks

Search and think [Inferential and interpretive comprehension]

1 What is meant by 'star-cross'd lovers'?
   a Fate destroys their chances of happiness.
   b The lovers are born under opposite star signs.
2 How long have the families been fighting?
   a A long time
   b For two hours
3 What might be meant by two families 'both alike in dignity'?
   a They have the same social status and importance.
   b Both families behave in a dignified way.
4 What is meant by 'death-mark'd love'?
5 Copy out the lines from the passage which mean a new fight has occurred and people have been killed.

Optional assessment: 5 x 1 mark = 5 marks

Hidden depths [Creative comprehension – responding personally, higher-order-thinking skills, making links]

1 What is the purpose of telling the play's outcome at the beginning?
2 What do families argue about?

Optional assessment: 2 x 2 marks = 4 marks

Extend yourself [Links to real life or other literature, researching, writing, creating, speaking tasks]

- Write a love story that would be of interest to your age group. Aim to create an obstacle that the lovers must overcome before they can be together.
- Write a dialogue between two lovers and act it out for the class.
- In pairs, put together a PowerPoint presentation of romance fiction book covers and analyse these for the class.

UNIT 7

In the science lab

TEXT TYPE Procedure/Instructions

PURPOSE To give instructions or show how something is accomplished through a series of steps

STRUCTURE
1 Opening statement of goal or aim
2 Material required listed in order of use
3 Series of steps listed in chronological order

FEATURES Logical sequence of steps, may use technical language and diagrams

Experiment 6.1 Sources of heat

How can we obtain heat?

In most cases, you can tell if heat is being produced by slowly bringing the back of your hand towards the likely source of heat.

1 ***Friction***

Rub your hands together; rub two pieces of wood together; saw a piece of wood; file some metal.

2 ***Chemical***

a Light a candle, light some methylated spirits in a lid, light a Bunsen burner.

b Add some dilute hydrochloric acid to dilute caustic soda (sodium hydroxide).

3 ***Electrical***

Plug in and turn on a radiator, connect some resistance wire to a battery, connect a lamp to a battery.

4 ***Sun***

Use a handlens to focus some light from the Sun either on some paper or onto a dead leaf.

DO NOT FOCUS THE LIGHT ONTO YOUR BODY
DO NOT LOOK AT THE SUN THROUGH A HANDLENS

On the surface [Literal comprehension – right-there questions]

1 List the four main sources of heat.
2 List the materials needed to produce heat chemically.
3 When using a handlens what should you not do?
4 How can you tell if heat is being produced?
5 What is the other name for caustic soda?

Optional assessment: 5 x 1 mark = 5 marks

Discovering techniques [Language structures and features, spelling, grammar, vocabulary]

1 List three features that indicate that this text consists of instructions or a procedure.

Optional assessment: 1 x 3 marks = 3 marks

Search and think [Inferential and interpretive comprehension]

1 List the sources of heat that can also produce fire.
2 Which source of heat involves heat being produced through movement?
3 Which source of heat is produced by connecting to a source of energy?
4 Explain the purpose of the handlens in producing heat.
5 Most sources of heat need a source of energy to produce heat. List the source of energy for friction.

Optional assessment: 5 x 1 mark = 5 marks

Hidden depths [Creative comprehension – responding personally, higher-order thinking skills, making links]

1 Which sources of heat do you use most often and for what purpose?
2 If the sources of heat you used most often were not available to you, which other sources would you use?

Optional assessment: 2 x 2 marks = 4 marks

Extend yourself [Links to real life or other literature, researching, writing, creating, speaking tasks]

- Complete the experiments and write a report.
- Research alternative energy sources and complete a poster about them.
- Select one of the experiments and present a demonstration to the class, instructing them on how to perform the experiment. (You may use PowerPoint.)
- Choose one of the experiments and draw a labelled diagram to explain how you would perform the experiment.

UNIT 8 Lights and mirrors

TEXT TYPE Explanation
PURPOSE To inform, to explain how or why things are as they are, or how things work
STRUCTURE
1 A general statement
2 Series of statement or events in chronological or logical order
3 Concluding statement
FEATURES Logical sequence of details or ideas may use heading, diagrams and tables

Mirror, mirror on the wall

'Mirror, mirror on the wall, who's the fairest of them all?' From ancient times, reflections from pools of water, polished stones and metallic objects were thought to be magical. Today, mirrors are used for many different purposes. We use them every day to see our reflection and to see behind us and around corners when we are cycling or driving, for example.

Light

To understand how mirrors produce images, we need to understand what light does, because it is light that brings images to our eyes. This light comes from many sources, such as the Sun, light bulbs and torch globes.

One of the most important properties of light is that it travels in straight lines. It leaves its source and travels in a straight line until it reaches another surface or the eye of the observer. You may have noticed that it does this if you shine a torch in a dark room.

Making a shadow

If there is something blocking the path of the light that the light cannot pass through, then it cannot reach the observer and a shadow is created. If light did not travel in straight lines there would be no such things as shadows.

Reflection

Another important thing that light does is that when it hits the surface of something, some or all of it bounces back, like a ball bouncing off a wall. Like the bouncing ball, as it travels back away from the surface it again moves in a straight line. We call this bouncing back reflection, and if it wasn't for this ability to reflect we could not see ourselves in a mirror.

On the surface [Literal comprehension – right-there questions]

1 From what did people long ago see reflections?
2 Give two examples of what we use mirrors for today.
3 What is one of the most important properties of light?
4 How can you test whether light travels in a straight line?
5 What can change the direction light travels in?

Optional assessment: 5 x 1 mark = 5 marks

Discovering techniques [Language structures and features, spelling, grammar, vocabulary]

1 Look up the following words in a dictionary and write out their meanings. Remember to keep in context with the passage.
   a fairest   b reflection   c polished   d metallic
   e magical   f images   g properties   h source
   i ability
2 Why has the author chosen to use subheadings?

Optional assessment: 10 x 1 mark = 10 marks

Search and think [Inferential and interpretive comprehension]

1 How are shadows formed?
2 What does the fact that we can see ourselves in a mirror prove?
3 Which of the following statements is true?
   a Light keeps going in the same line for ever.
   b If light did not go in straight lines we would not see our image in a mirror.
   c When light hits surfaces, all of it always bounces back.
   d Only mirrors can produce reflections.
4 How does the existence of shadows prove that light travels in straight lines?
5 If light could pass through everything, would you ever get shadows?

Optional assessment: 5 x 1 mark = 5 marks

Hidden depths [Creative comprehension – responding personally, higher-order-thinking skills, making links]

1 Why do you think people in ancient times thought reflections were magical?
2 Make a list of the everyday uses you have for mirrors.

Optional assessment: 2 x 3 marks = 6 marks

Extend yourself [Links to real life or other literature, researching, writing, creating, speaking tasks]

- Conduct some experiments using a torch, a mirror, a light and a darkened room. Write a brief report on your findings.
- List all the stories you know of where mirrors or reflections with magical qualities feature, e.g. Snow White, Harry Potter, Narcissus. Explain what the characters saw in the mirror or reflection that was so important.
- Whenever people look in a mirror, they not only see what they look like but they are also aware that the reflection shows what other people see. Try putting on your grumpiest face while looking at yourself in the mirror. Now try your happiest face. Write an account of how different you looked.

UNIT 9 Out in space

TEXT TYPE	Narrative – science fiction
PURPOSE	To tell a story; includes a basis of scientific fact or theory
STRUCTURE	1 Orientation – fictional who or what, where and when (fantasy world) 2 Complication, damaged world/environment 3 Series of events to save the world/ survive 4 Resolution
FEATURES	Use of past tense, pronouns, technical or scientific language

From *Rocket Ship Galileo* by Robert A Heinlein

'Goshawmighty,' exclaimed Art, 'this is something!'

He unlimbered his equipment and began snapping frantically, until Ross pointed out that his lens cover was still on. Then he steadied down. Ross floated face down and stared out at the desolation. They were speeding silently along, only two hundred miles above the ground, and they were approaching the sunrise line of light and darkness. The shadows were long on the barren wastes below them, the mountain peaks and the great gaping craters more horrendous on that account. 'It's scary,' Ross decided. 'I'm not sure I like it.'

'Want off at the next corner?' Cargraves inquired.

'No, but I'm not dead certain I'm glad I came.'

Morrie grasped his arm, to steady himself apparently, but quite as much for the comfort of solid human companionship. 'You know what I think, Ross,' he began, as he stared out at the endless miles of craters. 'I think I know how it got that way. Those aren't volcanic craters, that's certain – and it wasn't done by meteors. They did it themselves!'

'Huh? Who?'

'The moon people. They did it. They wrecked themselves. They ruined themselves. They had one atomic war too many.'

'Huh? What the – ' Ross stared, then looked back at the surface as if to read the grim mystery there.

Art stopped taking pictures.

'How about it, Doc?'

Cargraves wrinkled his brow. 'Could be,' he admitted. 'None of the other theories for natural causes hold water for one reason or another. It would account for the relatively smooth parts we call 'seas'.

'They really were seas; that's why they weren't hit very hard.'

'And that's why they aren't seas any more,' Morrie went on. 'They blew their atmosphere off and the seas boiled away. Look at Tycho. That's where they set off the biggest ammunition dump on the planet. I'll bet somebody worked out a counter-weapon that worked too well. It set off every atom bomb on the moon all at once and it ruined them! I'm sure of it.'

'Well,' said Cargraves, 'I'm not sure of it, but I admit the theory is attractive. Perhaps we'll find out when we land.'

On the surface [Literal comprehension – right-there questions]

1 What is the name of the rocket ship?
2 What are they floating 200 miles above?
3 What do they see?
4 List the people who are on the ship.
5 What is Ross's theory as to how the craters got there?

Optional assessment: 5 x 1 mark = 5 marks

Discovering techniques [Language structures and features, spelling, grammar, vocabulary]

1 Look up the following words in a dictionary and write out their meanings. Remember to keep in context with the passage.
   a desolation
   b barren
   c horrendous
   d meteors
2 What does the phrase 'doesn't hold water' mean?
3 Because this extract is mostly dialogue you get many examples of colloquial language. List as many as you can find.

Optional assessment: 3 x 2 marks = 6 marks

Search and think [Inferential and interpretive comprehension]

1 According to the story, which place has the biggest ammunition dump on the planet?
2 Why do the men believe the craters weren't created by natural causes?
   a They weren't volcanic
   b They weren't created by meteors
   c Both of the above
3 What evidence supports their theory that the moon people ruined themselves?
   a They had one atomic war too many
   b The desolation
   c The relatively smooth parts called the seas
4 Explain what happened to the seas.
5 What do you think Cargraves needs to do before he will be sure of Ross's theory?

Optional assessment: 5 x 1 mark = 5 marks

Hidden depths [Creative comprehension – responding personally, higher-order thinking skills, making links]

1 What do you think has happened to the moon people?
2 How do the men feel about landing on the moon? What do you think they will find there?

Optional assessment: 2 x 2 marks = 4 marks

Extend yourself [Links to real life or other literature, researching, writing, creating, speaking tasks]

- Find out about the effects of atomic/nuclear bombs, particularly at Hiroshima and Nagasaki.
- Read another book about the result of nuclear holocausts (perhaps as part of your wider reading programme). Write a book review and share it with the other members of your class. You may like to choose one of the following.
  - *Z for Zachariah* by Robert O'Brien
  - *The Last Children* by Gudrun Pausewang
  - *Children of the Dust* by Louise Lawrence
  - *Hiroshima* by John Hersey
  - *Obernewtyn* by Isabelle Carmody

UNIT 10 It's a 'bad' thing

TEXT TYPE Thesaurus
PURPOSE To aid the expression of ideas in writing, to increase vocabulary
STRUCTURE 1 Alphabetical
2 Slang and informal words included.
FEATURES Abbreviations, font changes

From *The Oxford Student's Thesaurus*

bad adj. **1.** *Bad person or deed.* abhorrent, abominable, atrocious, awful, base, beastly, corrupt, despicable, detestable, dishonest, evil, hateful, immoral, infamous, loathsome, malevolent, malicious, mean, naughty, notorious, sinful, undesirable, ungodly, unkind, unrighteous, unworthy, vile, villainous, wicked. SEE ALSO **cruel**. OPP. good. **2.** *bad weather*. appalling (inf.), atrocious (inf.), foul, lousy (sl.), shocking (inf.), terrible, unpleasant. OPP. fair, fine. **3.** *bad conditions*. abysmal, adverse, appalling (inf.), deplorable, hopeless, pitiful, unfavourable, unpleasant, woeful. **4.** *It was a bad accident*. appalling, awful, dire, disastrous, dreadful, frightful, ghastly, hideous, horrible, horrific, horrifying, nasty, serious, severe, shocking, terrible. OPP. minor, slight. **5.** *The food had been left out of the refrigerator and was all bad*. decayed, foul, mildewed, mouldy, off, putrid, rotten, spoiled, tainted. OPP. fresh. **6.** *a bad smell*. foul, offensive, on the nose (Austral. sl.), revolting, stinking, vile. OPP. fragrant, pleasant. **7.** *bad workmanship*. defective, faulty, incompetent, inferior, poor, shoddy, unsatisfactory, unsound, worthless. OPP good. **8.** *a bad business*. **9.** *She always feels bad*. crook (Austral. & NZ sl.), ill, off colour, poorly, sick, unhealthy, unwell. OPP. fine. **10.** *Sweets are bad for your teeth*. damaging, deleterious, destructive, harmful, hurtful, ruinous, undesirable, unhealthy. OPP good. **bad blood** enmity. **bad language** abuse, expletives, invective, obscenities, swearwords, vituperation. **bad-tempered** adj. angry, crook (Austral. & NZ sl.), cross, hot-tempered, ill-tempered, maggoty (Austral. sl.)

On the surface [Literal comprehension – right-there questions]

1 The topics for the adjective 'bad' are numbered and written in italics. Write out the topics.
2 Adjectives are describing words. The adjectives for '*bad person*' are listed.
  a in order of importance
  b in order of relevance
  c alphabetically
3 What are the opposite words for 'bad accident'?
4 What is the 'SEE ALSO' word given for bad person or deed?
5 Slang is highly informal colloquial language. Often slang conveys negative connotations. List two slang words used to describe bad weather.

Optional assessment: 5 x 1 mark = 5 marks

Discovering techniques [Language structures and features, spelling, grammar, vocabulary]

1 Look up 'bad' in the dictionary. Write out the definition. How is the definition similar or different to the entry in the thesaurus?
2 A thesaurus uses many abbreviations. Write the following addreviations out in full:
  adj. inf. sl. Austral. OPP.

Optional assessment: 2 x 3 marks = 6 marks

Search and think [Inferential and interpretive comprehension]

1 Using the words listed for 'bad', describe food that has been left out of the refrigerator and now smells bad.
2 List behaviour which could be described as 'base'. (See the first definition.)
3 Write a short paragraph, using the words listed, to describe bad weather and bad driving conditions which result in a bad accident.
4 Find two words in the list which describe a person who has a reputation for bad behaviour.
5 Make a list of words which describe mild bad behaviour and those which are high-level bad behaviour.

Optional assessment: 5 x 1 mark = 5 marks

Hidden depths [Creative comprehension – responding personally, higher-order thinking skills, making links]

1 Describe an experience when you have been bad, or you have witnessed someone being bad. Outline what happened and use one of the adjectives listed to describe the behaviour.
2 Discuss in small groups a notorious/infamous person. What did he or she do? Which words could you use to describe this person's behaviour?

Optional assessment: 2 x 2 marks = 4 marks

Extend yourself [Links to real life or other literature, researching, writing, creating, speaking tasks]

- Research an infamous or notorious person or couple, e.g. Bonnie and Clyde, Ronald Biggs, Ned Kelly, Hitler, Stalin, Pol Pot, Billy the Kid, Minnie Dean. Write a report about who they were, what they did. Use words from the list to describe their behaviour. Try to explain why their deeds have made them infamous/notorious.

UNIT 11

Which book?

TEXT TYPE	Book review
PURPOSE	To give details and opinion on a text
STRUCTURE	Review 1 Context – background information on the text. Details of author (other texts, prizes, etc.) 2 Description of the text (including characters and plot) 3 Intended audience 4 Concluding statement (judgement, opinion or recommendation)
FEATURES	Language may be formal or informal depending on purpose and audience, may include examples and quotes, publisher and price

From *The Summer Book Guide*

ROVER SAVES CHRISTMAS

Roddy Doyle SCHOLASTIC PRESS $24.95 HC

You don't remember Rover? Well, you ought to. The hero of last year's adventure, *The Giggler Treatment*, Rover is a rather amazing dog. He can poo on command, can travel at supersonic speed, and has made a fortune exploiting his talents. It's Christmas Eve in Dublin and disaster is looming. Jimmy and Robby Mack are so desperate for Santa's arrival that they've made twenty-seven sandwiches for Santa and peeled carrots for Rudolph. But there's a big problem. Rudolph is off sick and the sleigh is grounded. Can Rover save the day for Jimmy, Robby and millions of other boys and girls? Roddy Doyle, author of the Booker Prize-winning *Paddy Clarke Ha, Ha, Ha* shows his remarkable ability to write rude and hilarious kids' books.

THE HOSTILE HOSPITAL: A SERIES OF UNFORTUNATE EVENTS, BOOK THE EIGHTH

Lemony Snicket HARPERCOLLINS $17.95 HC

Those poor, pathetic Baudelaire Orphans! Just when you think things couldn't get any worse for them, our narrator finds more hard times for Violet, Klaus and Sunny. According to Lemony Snicket, 'This book ... describes every last detail of the Baudelaire children's miserable stay at Heimlich Hospital, which makes it one of the most dreadful books in the world. There are many pleasant things to read about, but this book contains none of them.' Now clearly this makes the reviewer's task that much more difficult. Imagine trying to say something nice about the awful lives of these nice children? Perhaps you'd like to try yourselves?

Also available: *The Bad Beginning* (1), *The Reptile Room* (2), *The Wide Window* (3), *The Miserable Mill* (4), *The Austere Academy* (5), *The Ersatz Elevator* (6), *The Vile Village* (7).

COUNTING CROCODILES

Judy Sierra Illustrated by Will Hillenbrand VOYAGER $16.75 PB

'The Sillabobble crocodiles thought they were truly cool, and they looked upon those waters as their private swimming pool. They appeared to be quite vicious, feasting fearlessly on fishes.' Poor monkey. All she has to eat are sour lemons. One day she spies a banana tree on a faraway island, but the only way to get there is to navigate the crocodile-infested waters of the Sillabobble Sea. That's no problem when you're a brave, clever monkey who knows how to count to ten and back. Bright, full colour, very funny illustrations to complement the text make this a must for the pre-school set.

On the surface [Literal comprehension – right-there questions]

1 Name the title of the previous year's Rover text by Roddy Doyle.
2 List another text Roddy Doyle has written and the prize he has been given.
3 What is the surname of the children in Lemony Snicket's book?
4 Who is the intended audience for *Counting Crocodiles*?

Optional assessment: 4 x 1 mark = 4 marks

Discovering techniques [Language structures and features, spelling, grammar, vocabulary]

1 Look up the following words in a dictionary and write out their meanings. Remember to keep in context with the passage.
   a exploiting b looming c hilarious
   d pathetic e miserable
2 Alliteration is the repetition of the same sound at the beginning of words, usually appearing in the same sentence, e.g. **P**remier **p**romotes **p**arty. Find an example of alliteration in each of the reviews.
3 What do the abbreviations HC and PB stand for?
4 The review of *Rover Saves Christmas* begins with what language technique?
5 Make a list of the words and phrases you think try to persuade you to buy the books.

Optional assessment: 9 x 1 mark = 9 marks

Search and think [Inferential and interpretive comprehension]

1 For which age group do you think *Rover Saves Christmas* is appropriate? Explain why.
2 What is the reviewer's opinion of *Rover Saves Christmas*? Write a quote of the reviewer's opinion.
3 Who do you think the intended audience is for these reviews?
4 What is the storyline for *A Series of Unfortunate Events*?
5 All the titles in Lemony Snicket's series have something in common. Explain what you think it is.

Optional assessment: 5 x 1 mark = 5 marks

Hidden depths [Creative comprehension – responding personally, higher-order thinking skills, making links]

1 Which book would you like to read? Explain what in particular appeals to you. If you do not like the sound of these books, explain why not.
2 Would you read a review such as this if you were looking to read or purchase a book for yourself or for a gift? Explain how it would be useful.
3 These reviews have all been written in a similar style. Read them again looking carefully at their structure, vocabulary choice and tone. Use the same style to write a review on a book you are currently reading. Alternatively you may like to use one of the sophisticated picture books from your school library. Reread the information in the box at the top of the previous page before you begin.

Optional assessment: 3 x 2 marks = 6 marks

Extend yourself [Links to real life or other literature, researching, writing, creating, speaking tasks]

- Visit either your local or your school library and locate one of the three books. Having read it, do you agree or disagree with the review?
- Do a web search to find the biography of one of the three authors.
- Create an advertising poster for one of the three books. Use the information from the review to help you.

UNIT 12 At the truck stop

TEXT TYPE	Description
PURPOSE	To describe the characteristic features of a particular thing
STRUCTURE	1 Opening statement – introduction to the subject 2 Characteristic features of the subject 3 Concluding comment (optional)
FEATURES	Details involving senses to assist readers to visualise a scene or event.

From *A Bridge to Wiseman's Cove* by James Moloney

Prelude

The lights of the service station created a circle of warmth and movement amid the darkness. Weary travellers pulled in from the highway, gathering like moths around a grimy bulb to refill the petrol tank, stretch aching muscles and hunch over a cup of tea for a few minutes in the all-night café. None of these travellers noticed a lonely figure who shunned the bright light to wait among the semitrailers parked at the edge of the tarmac. Only when a bus halted nearby, its air brakes hissing, the gravel crushed and crackling under the massive wheels, did the figure stir and creep to the corner of an enormous prime mover to watch as the passengers stepped down and wandered, yawning, into the café.

An elderly man was the last to leave. He lowered an arthritic leg gingerly from the bottom step, leaning heavily on the driver who waited patiently below. With this man safely on solid ground, the driver closed the door and headed off towards the lights in the wake of his passengers. The figure stepped from the darkness and tried the door. Locked.

Twenty minutes later the driver returned, leading this time an informal line of travellers at his back. With a quick twist of his key, the door folded open and he stood aside to let them pass. The stragglers would be a few moments yet so he climbed aboard, easing into the seat as they came in ones and twos. He didn't notice a woman step from the shadow of a removal van and close up behind a pair of sleepy teenagers. She mounted the steps, careful to keep the tell-tale knapsack concealed as best she could and continued down the bus, nonchalantly checking the webbed pockets behind each seat until she found an empty one. She slipped into the seat, then leaned forward, taking an age to tie and re-tie her shoelaces.

The front door sighed as it closed and the bus lurched forward, to pause briefly at the edge of the highway. A car swept past, leaving the road behind it suddenly black and empty. The driver gunned the engine, commanding its throaty roar and the bus pulled away from the road-house into the sea of darkness.

Only then did the woman sit up and permit herself a smile.

On the surface [Literal comprehension – right-there questions]

1 Where was the lonely figure waiting?
2 Where did the driver go during the twenty-minute break?
3 Who did the woman hide behind as she climbed in the bus?
4 What was the woman careful to keep concealed?
5 Why did the bus pause briefly at the edge of the tarmac?

Optional assessment: 5 x 1 mark = 5 marks

Discovering techniques [Language structures and features, spelling, grammar, vocabulary]

1 Look up the following words in a dictionary and write out their meanings. Remember to keep in context with the passage.
   a grimy   b shunned   c creep
   d gingerly   e nonchalantly
2 Which 'person' is the passage written in: first or third?
3 Is the passage written in the past or present tense?
4 Similes are comparisons that use the word 'like' or 'as', e.g. It was light as day. Find an example of a simile in the text.
5 a Descriptive writing should not only describe the setting and behaviour of people in the text, it should also capture the mood or sense of what it was like to be in that place at that time. List the sounds described in the passage.
   b The passage has many images (word pictures) that help us 'see' the scene. List the images.
   c Smell is one sense not included. Describe the smells that would relate to this passage.

Optional assessment: 12 x 1 mark = 12 marks

Search and think [Inferential and interpretive comprehension]

1 How does the writer establish early in the passage that the woman is hiding?
2 Why did she check the web-pockets?
3 What time of day do you think the passage is set in? Quote from the text to back up your choice.
4 Make a list of words used in the passage to describe the woman's behaviour. What impression do they give of her?
5 Why didn't the driver notice her before the bus took off?
6 Why did she 'permit herself a smile'?

Optional assessment: 6 x 1 mark = 6 marks

Hidden depths [Creative comprehension – responding personally, higher-order-thinking skills, making links]

1 Write (or draw) your own description of the woman. Explain what she looks like, what she is wearing, and so on.
2 How effective is the passage in capturing your attention? Do you want to keep on reading? What do you want to know?

Optional assessment: 2 x 2 marks = 4 marks

Extend yourself [Links to real life or other literature, researching, writing, creating, speaking tasks]

- Where is the 'lonely figure' from this extract going? Write your own story following on from this passage. Decide if you will continue in the third person. You may decide to slip into the first person, becoming the woman on the bus or someone else on the bus. Start with the next 'scene'. Remember to include sights and sounds, e.g. action: shrunk, curled, collapsed into the seat; face: smiled, frowned, wrinkled.

UNIT 13 Stand clear

TEXT TYPE Poem
PURPOSE To express ideas in precise and powerful language
STRUCTURE Stanzas
FEATURES Careful word choice for meaning and sound, figurative language, verse, rhyme, imagery

Death of a tree
by Jack Davis

The power saw screamed
then turned to a muttering.
She leaned forward,
fell.
A sad abruptness
in the limpness of foliage,
in the final folding of limbs.
I placed my hand on what was left:
one hundred years of graceful beauty ended,
and the underside of leaves pale
blended with the morning rain.
Better for her to have been overpowered
by wind or storm.
That would have been a battle,
a fitter end for such a forest giant
than this ignoble inevitability
because man was involved.
Man is pain.
I walked away and left her,
saddened,
aware of my loss.
Yet – still,
part of the gain.

On the surface [Literal comprehension – right-there questions]

1 Explain in three or four sentences what the poem is about.
2 How old was the tree?
3 How does the poet feel about the situation?
4 According to the poet, what would have been a better end for the tree?
5 Give one example of the way the tree is given human qualities.

Optional assessment: 5 x 1 mark = 5 marks

Discovering techniques [Language structures and features, spelling, grammar, vocabulary]

1 Look up the following words in a dictionary and write out their meanings. Remember to keep in context with the passage.
   a muttering b abruptness c inevitability
2 Personification involves giving inanimate objects human qualities. Write a one-paragraph description of your house using personification. For example, is it a tired house, an energetic house? Does the gate sing when you open it?

Optional assessment: 2 x 3 marks = 6 marks

Search and think [Inferential and interpretive comprehension]

1 What is the effect of the title?
2 Why might the poet have used the word 'screamed'?
3 List words or phrases that create a mood of sadness.
4 What is the message of the poem?
5 What does the poet mean when he writes, 'still, part of the gain'?

Optional assessment: 5 x 2 marks = 10 marks

Hidden depths [Creative comprehension – responding personally, higher-order-thinking skills, making links]

1 Do you believe New Zealanders respect the environment? Give reasons for your response.
2 Write a poem about the environment. This should be ten lines. You could write about your local area, your school or a place you feel is under threat in the world.

Optional assessment: 2 x 5 marks = 10 marks

Extend yourself [Links to real life or other literature, researching, writing, creating, speaking tasks]

- Create an anthology of poems which have the environment as a theme. Illustrate these with your own drawings.
- Read more of the works of Jack Davis. Research his life and write a report.

UNIT 14 Knights on horseback

TEXT TYPE Historical report
PURPOSE To reconstruct past experiences by retelling events in the order in which they occurred
STRUCTURE
1 Orientation – background information about who, where and when
2 Series of events in chronological order
3 A personal comment
FEATURES Use of past tense, action verbs, descriptive language, may include quotes

Becoming a knight

Knights had a high position in medieval society. Because conditions were often violent and unsettled, military power was very important. The knights were a warrior elite, and their status in society reflected this importance.

A warrior elite

Knights fought on horseback as cavalry troops. The cavalry were the most important troops in medieval armies. Their armour, equipment and war-horses were very expensive, and few people could afford them. At great fairs in Champagne in the thirteenth century, for example, war-horses were sold for about £85 each. It would take an ordinary foot-soldier 32 years to earn that amount of money.

Becoming a knight

The sons of knights were sent to the household of another knight at about the age of twelve to learn the skills of knighthood. They were trained by serving the knight in many ways – by grooming his horses and looking after his armour, for example. A young man who served a knight in this way was called a 'squire'. Squires also learned to ride and fight on horseback, and to look after weapons. One skill considered particularly important was how to serve the lord with food at table.

By the thirteenth century complicated ceremonies had developed to mark the occasion on which a man finally became a knight. On the day before the ceremony, the knight-to-be took a special bath, and then dressed in white clothes. He spent the night in prayer in church, kneeling in front of the altar on which his sword and armour lay. Early the next morning mass was said in church, then the knight was dressed in his armour. Prayers were said over the armour and sword. These were intended to dedicate the knight and his work to God. Finally another knight dealt him a blow on the neck with his hand or sword. The new knight vowed to act according to the code of chivalry.

On the surface [Literal comprehension – right-there questions]

1 What position did knights have in medieval society?
2 Which were the most important troops in medieval armies?
3 What could few people afford to buy?
4 Who would be sent to the household of a knight to learn the skills of knighthood?
5 List the duties a 'squire' (knight in training) would be expected to learn.

Optional assessment: 5 x 1 mark = 5 marks

Discovering techniques [Language structures and features, spelling, grammar, vocabulary]

1 Find out the meaning of 'chivalry'.
2 Find out the meaning of the word 'elite'. Who do you believe are the elite of our society today?

Optional assessment: 2 x 2 marks = 4 marks

Search and think [Inferential and interpretive comprehension]

1 Why do you think the sons of knights trained under another knight rather than their fathers?
2 Devise a chart which outlines in detail the two-day procedure for becoming a knight.
3 To whom does the knight dedicate himself in the ceremony?
4 Why did knights have such a high position in medieval society?
5 War-horses were sold for 85 pounds each in the thirteenth century. If it took an ordinary foot soldier 32 years to earn that amount of money, calculate how much he would earn a year.

Optional assessment: 5 x 1 mark = 5 marks

Hidden depths [Creative comprehension – responding personally, higher-order-thinking skills, making links]

Research the 'Code of Chivalry' before you answer the following questions.

1 Write an advertisement for a new squire. List the qualities that you require. Alternatively, write an advertisement for a 'Knight in Shining Armour'.
2 Who are the 'warrior elite' in today's military? Outline the skills these people would need to have. Include personal qualities a soldier needs. You may like to visit one of the New Zealand Defence Forces websites before you begin.
3 You are a 12-year-old squire who has just started his training. Write a letter home describing your experiences.

Optional assessment: 3 x 3 marks = 9 marks

Extend yourself [Links to real life or other literature, researching, writing, creating, speaking tasks]

- Make your own coat of arms. Include four symbols that tell something about your family, background, environment and personal interests.
- Research famous knights. Write a report on your findings.
- View some of the latest films about knights (e.g. *A Knight's Tale*, *Black Knight*, *Joan of Arc*), or view some old classics (e.g. *The Holy Grail*, *Excalibur*) and write a review.
- Read novels about knights and life in medieval times: Catherine Jinks has written a series set in medieval times: *Pagan's Crusade*, *Pagan's Scribe*, *Pagan in Exile*, *Pagan's Vows*.
  More advanced readers might try: *Mammoth Book of Arthurian Legends* edited by Mike Ashley; *The Winter King* by Bernard Cornwell; *Mists of Avalon* by Marion Zimmer Bradley; Tennyson's '*Morte d'Arthur*'.
- Devise an obstacle course for knights in training.

UNIT 15

Sailing the world

TEXT TYPE Map
PURPOSE To show locations and features
STRUCTURE Pictorial representation of a region
FEATURES Visual information, combining words, symbols and images

Jesse's voyage

Redrawn from Jesse Martin (with Ed Gannon), *Lionheart: A Journey of the Human Spirit*.

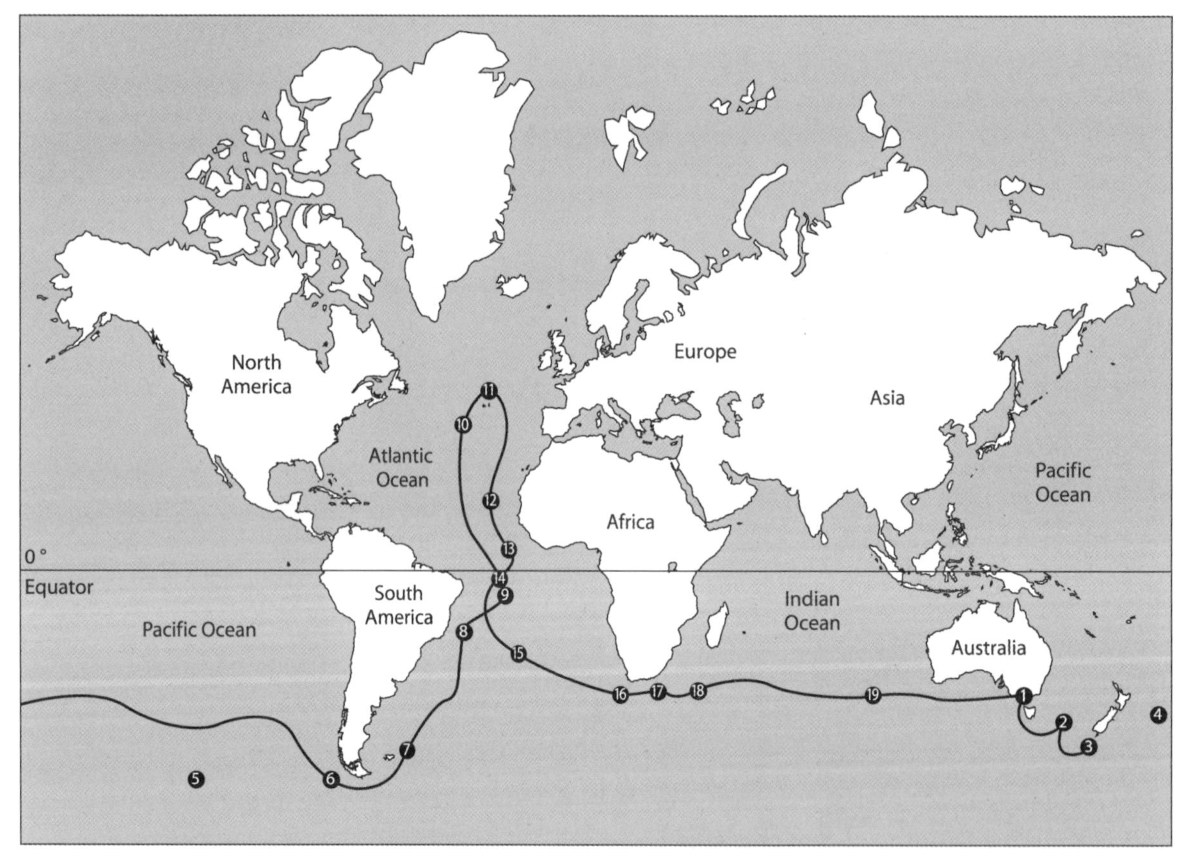

On the surface [Literal comprehension – right-there questions]

1 Whose journey does the map depict?
2 When did he depart?
3 Where did he depart from?
4 When did he arrive home?
5 How many times did Jesse cross the equator?

Optional assessment: 5 x 1 mark = 5 marks

Discovering techniques [Language structures and features, spelling, grammar, vocabulary]

Geography skills

1 In which direction did Jesse sail?
2 In which hemisphere was Jesse for most of his journey?
3 Using an atlas, work out where Jesse met his family.

Nautical terms

4 What happens when you are 'becalmed'?
5 Find out what a 'force 10 storm' is. Summarise the scale and outline how bad this would have been for Jesse.

Optional assessment: 5 x 1 mark = 5 marks

Search and think [Inferential and interpretive comprehension]

1 What does the key show?
2 How many days did it take Jesse to sail from Victoria to where he celebrated Christmas Day?
3 In which ocean did Jesse have the least problems?
4 Which part of the journey do you think was the most dangerous?
5 Why do you think Jesse met up with his family where he did?

Optional assessment: 5 x 1 mark = 5 marks

Hidden depths [Creative comprehension – responding personally, higher-order-thinking skills, making links]

1 How do you think Jesse spent his eighteenth birthday? Write his diary entry for this day.

Optional assessment: 1 x 2 marks = 2 marks

Extend yourself [Links to real life or other literature, researching, writing, creating, speaking tasks]

- Undertake research about modern-day piracy. On a map, mark the areas where there are piracy problems. Write a report on what happens and how the authorities are attempting to deal with it.
- Read Jesse's book *Lionheart: A Journey of the Human Spirit*. Write a brief summary of the 19 events noted on the map. Write a report of what happened, where he was and what he did.
- View the film *White Squall* on video.

UNIT 16 Graphic information

TEXT TYPE	Pictograph
PURPOSE	Visual communication of information
STRUCTURE	1 Pictures/images/signs 2 Symbols 3 Illustrations 4 Tables
FEATURES	Statistical information presented as a graphic illustration, visually accurate relationship between the picture and figures presented

Transportation and the atmosphere

	Number of passengers per automobile, bus or carriage	Number of kilometres per person per litre of fuel
		132.5 541.3
		757
		829

On the surface [Literal comprehension – right-there questions]

1 What are the three modes of transport shown in the chart?
2 What do the two other columns in the graph show?
3 What is the title of the chart?
4 Does the chart tell us anything about the atmosphere?
5 How many passengers are accounted for on the bus? How many on the train?

Optional assessment: 5 x 1 mark = 5 marks

Discovering techniques [Language structures and features, spelling, grammar, vocabulary]

1 The original form of this graph used gallons and miles in place of litres and kilometres. Find out the following.
   a Name a country that uses the terms 'gallon' and 'mile'.
   b Which is greater: a litre or a gallon, and by how much?
   c Which is greater, a kilometre or a mile, and by how much?
2 You will often read texts with American spelling. Find out the American spelling for 'kilometre' and 'litre', and list any spelling variations you might know between American English and New Zealand English.

Optional assessment: 2 x 3 marks = 6 marks

Search and think [Inferential and interpretive comprehension]

1 How many kilometres can one person travel per gallon of fuel when travelling by train?
2 How many kilometres can one person travel per gallon of fuel when there are four passengers in a car?
3 What is the graph 'telling' us about the effect of certain modes of transport on the atmosphere?
4 If travelling by car, what does the chart suggest you should do?
5 Which mode of transport is the most environmentally friendly?

Optional assessment: 5 x 1 mark = 5 marks

Hidden depths [Creative comprehension – responding personally, higher-order-thinking skills, making links]

1 List any current government policies that encourage fuel efficiency. If you can't think of any, suggest some strategies to encourage people to be more fuel-efficient in regard to transportation.
2 Which modes of transport do you mainly use? List the advantages/disadvantages of each.

Optional assessment: 2 x 2 marks = 4 marks

Extend yourself [Links to real life or other literature, researching, writing, creating, speaking tasks]

- Make a poster encouraging people to use public transport or to car-pool.
- Research and write a report about the effect of pollution on the atmosphere. Present this as a chart/poster.
- Find a map of train and bus lines in your city. Plan a trip from home to school, the city or a friend's place. How much would it cost? What do you need to know to get there?

UNIT 17 Acid rain

TEXT TYPE	Explanation – geography
PURPOSE	To inform and explain how or why things are as they are, or how things work
STRUCTURE	1 A general statement 2 A series of statements in chronological or logical order 3 Concluding statement
FEATURES	Logical sequence of details or ideas, may use headings, diagrams and tables

Kicking the coal habit

Coal-burning power plants are the main source of the air pollution that causes acid rain. Every year, the power plants of the world puff out more that 66 million tons of sulphur dioxides into the air through their smokestacks.

Many years ago, the air around the power plants was extremely polluted. Then, the power companies had an idea. They made their smokestacks much taller – as tall as skyscrapers – and the smoke just blew away with the wind. But this didn't really solve the problem. The wind just blew the pollution into somebody else's air.

To stop acid rain, power plants need to cut back on pollution, not just send it farther away. One way to do this is to clean the smoke before it comes out of the smokestacks. This is done with machines called scrubbers. In many countries, such as Japan, all new power plants and factories must be built with scrubbers. Many old plants, however, do not have scrubbers yet because they are costly to install.

London's killer smog

When too much pollution collects in the air, it can be dangerous. In 1952, weather patterns over the city of London prevented smoke from coal fires from blowing away. The smoke mixed with fog. Londoners invented a new word for it: smog. The thick smog made breathing almost impossible. More than 4000 people suffocated from breathing in this polluted air.

On the surface [Literal comprehension – right-there questions]

1 What is the main source of air pollution causing acid rain?
2 How many tons of sulphur dioxide are puffed into the air each year?
3 In order to stop acid rain, what do power plants need to do?
4 Why don't old power plants have scrubbers?
5 Who invented the word 'smog'?

Optional assessment: 5 x 1 mark = 5 marks

Discovering techniques [Language structures and features, spelling, grammar, vocabulary]

1 Find out about acid rain. Write a brief summary of your findings.
2 What is sulphur dioxide? Write a brief explanation.
3 Explain what 'sustainability' means. Make a poster or present a PowerPoint presentation to your class.

Optional assessment: 3 x 2 marks = 6 marks

Search and think [Inferential and interpretive comprehension]

1 How did power companies clear up the pollution around the power plants?
2 Why don't many power companies want to make the change from coal to other sources of energy?
3 What will be the effect of their refusal to change?
4 How is smog formed?
5 How is smog dangerous to people? Give an example of when this has happened.

Optional assessment: 5 x 1 mark = 5 marks

Hidden depths [Creative comprehension – responding personally, higher-order-thinking skills, making links]

1 Write a letter to the Prime Minister, giving your thoughts on coal-burning power plants.

Optional assessment: 1 x 3 marks = 3 marks

Extend yourself [Links to real life or other literature, researching, writing, creating, speaking tasks]

- Find out about the Kyoto Protocol. (You can search on the Internet or do a newspaper article search.) Find out what the New Zealand Government's involvement was/is in this.
- Research and present a report on alternative energy sources such as hydroelectricity, solar, wind or wave energy. What are the advantages/disadvantages?
- Research acid rain, particularly in Europe and the USA. How are the governments in these countries trying to save the forests?
- Find out the history and current status of coal-burning power stations in New Zealand.

UNIT 18 Harry's family

TEXT TYPE Narrative
PURPOSE To tell a story
STRUCTURE
1 Orientation – who or what, where and when
2 Complication
3 Series of events
4 Resolution
FEATURES Use of past tense, pronouns

The Mirror of Erised from *Harry Potter and the Philosopher's Stone* by JK Rowling

It was a magnificent mirror, as high as the ceiling, with an ornate gold frame, standing on two clawed feet. There was an inscription carved around the top: *Erised stra ehru oyt ube cafru oyt on wohsi.*

His panic fading now that there was no sound of Filch and Snape, Harry moved nearer to the mirror, wanting to look at himself but saw no reflection again. He stepped in front of it.

He had to clap his hands to his mouth to stop himself screaming. He whirled around. His heart was pounding far more furiously than when the book had screamed – for he had seen not only himself in the mirror, but a whole crowd of people standing right behind him.

But the room was empty. Breathing very fast, he turned slowly back to the mirror.

There he was, reflected in it, white and scared-looking, and there, reflected behind him, were at least ten others. Harry looked over his shoulder – but, still, no one was there. Or were they all invisible too? Was he in fact in a room full of invisible people and this mirror's trick was that it reflected them, invisible or not?

He looked in the mirror again. A woman standing right behind his reflection was smiling at him and waving. He reached out a hand and felt the air behind him. If she was really there, he'd touch her, their reflections were so close together, but he felt only air – she and the others existed only in the mirror. She was a very pretty woman. She had dark red hair and her eyes – her eyes are just like mine, Harry thought, edging a little closer to the glass. Bright green – exactly the same shape, but then he noticed that she was crying; smiling, but crying at the same time. The tall, thin, black-haired man standing next to her put his arm around her. He wore glasses, and his hair was very untidy. It stuck up at the back, just like Harry's did.

Harry was so close to the mirror now that his nose was nearly touching that of his reflection.

'Mum?' he whispered. 'Dad?'

They just looked at him, smiling. And slowly, Harry looked into the faces of the other people in the mirror and saw other pairs of green eyes like his, other noses like his, even a little old man who looked as though he had Harry's knobbly knees – Harry was looking at his family, for the first time in his life.

The Potters smiled and waved at Harry and he stared hungrily back at them, his hands pressed flat against the glass as though he was hoping to fall right through it and reach them. He had a powerful kind of ache inside him, half joy, half terrible sadness.

On the surface [Literal comprehension – right-there questions]

1 What is the inscription carved around the top of the mirror?
2 Why does Harry clap his hands to his mouth?
3 What does Harry's reflection look like in the mirror?
4 What does Harry notice about the woman with the dark red hair?
5 What does Harry whisper into the mirror?

Optional assessment: 5 x 1 mark = 5 marks

Discovering techniques [Language structures and features, spelling, grammar, vocabulary]

1 Look carefully at the following sentence and identify the parts of speech which follow.

> It was a magnificent mirror, as high as the ceiling, with an ornate gold frame, standing on two clawed feet.

noun (4) adjective (5) verb (1) pronoun (1) preposition (1)

Optional assessment: 5 x 1 mark = 5 marks

Search and think [Inferential and interpretive comprehension]

1 Is Harry invisible?
2 Why does Harry think he is in a room of invisible people?
3 Why was the woman smiling and crying?
4 Can you explain Harry's joy and intense sadness? How is it possible to feel both at the same time? Explain what you know or believe has happened.
5 Why did Harry not instantly recognise the people in the mirror as his family?
6 What do you think is meant by the words 'stared hungrily'?

Optional assessment: 6 x 1 mark = 6 marks

Hidden depths [Creative comprehension – responding personally, higher-order-thinking skills, making links]

1 Have you ever felt happy and sad at the same time? If you have, explain what happened.

Optional assessment: 1 x 2 marks = 2 marks

Extend yourself [Links to real life or other literature, researching, writing, creating, speaking tasks]

- Watch one or more of the Harry Potter films.
- Read the Harry Potter books. Compare the books with the films.
- Read reviews of the films/books. Write your own review.
- Script a conversation between Harry and his parents. What would they say to each other?
- If you enjoyed Harry Potter, you may like to read other books which have mystery and magic. Further reading includes:
  - The *Narnia* series by CS Lewis
  - *The Seeing Stone* by Kevin Crossley-Holland
  - *Holes* by Louis Sacher
  - *His Dark Materials* by Phillip Pullman.

UNIT 19 Promises, promises

TEXT TYPE Advertisement

PURPOSE To persuade by putting forward an argument or particular point of view, to sell a product

STRUCTURE (VARIES)
1 Images
2 Written or spoken language
3 Sensory appeal – e.g. colour, shape, music

FEATURES May include images, facts and figures, logical reasoning, examples, and persuasive or emotive language

Thursday Plantation acne treatment products

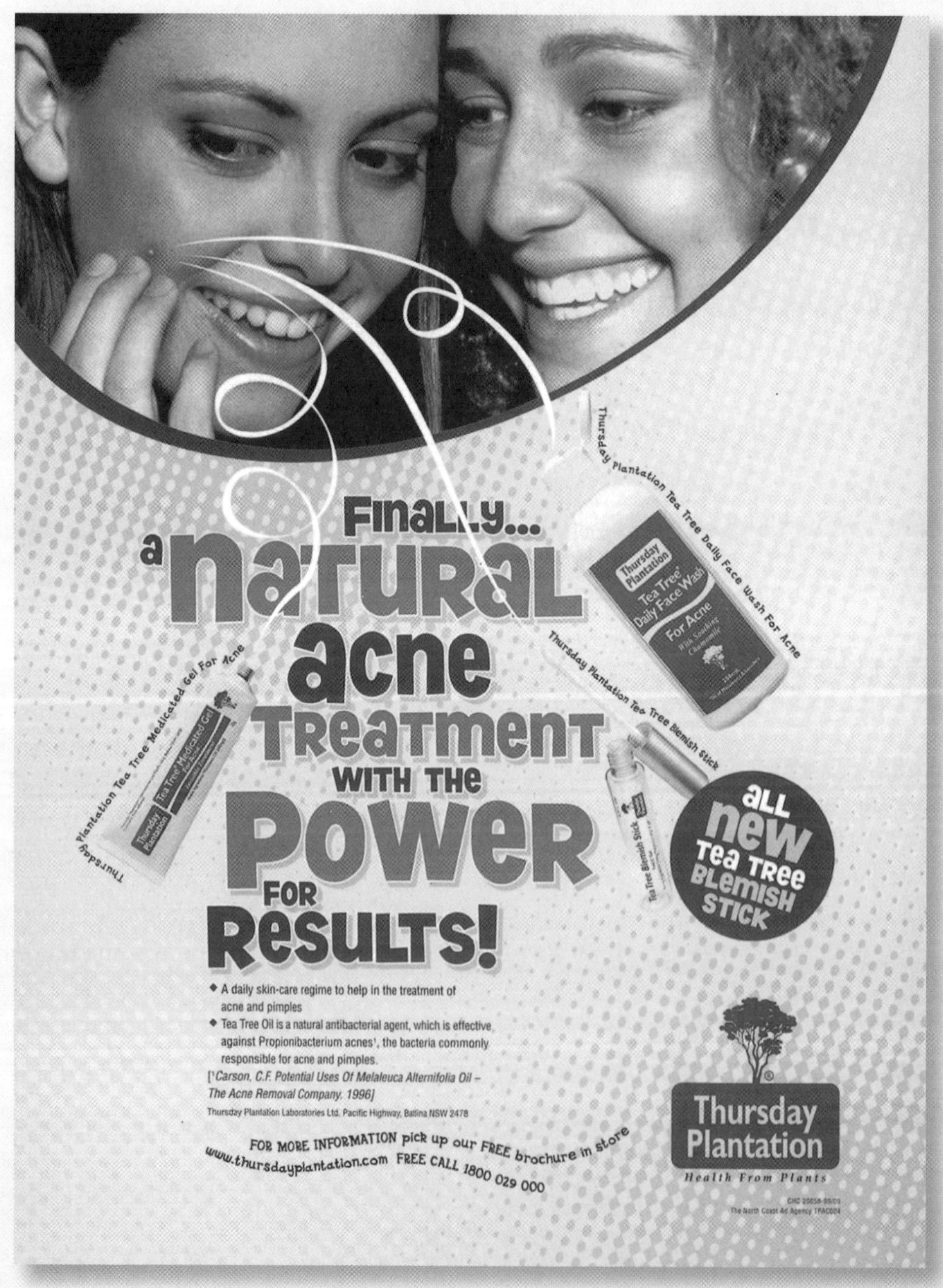

On the surface [Literal comprehension – right-there questions]

1 How many products are being advertised?
2 List the products being advertised.
3 What is the purpose of the products advertised here?
4 Which company makes these products?
5 What is the special ingredient in these products that differentiates them from other similar products?

Optional assessment: 5 x 1 mark = 5 marks

Discovering techniques [Language structures and features, spelling, grammar, vocabulary]

1 How many font styles and sizes are used in this advertisement? Why?
2 Would a photograph of the products themselves be more or less effective advertising? Why?

Optional assessment: 2 x 2 marks = 4 marks

Search and think [Inferential and interpretive comprehension]

1 What is the slogan of the company which manufactures these products and what does it imply?
2 Which words are emphasised in this advertisement? Why?
3 Why is the term 'regime' used?
4 How can you obtain more information about these products and why is this information mostly free?
5 Discuss three ways this advertisement attempts to appeal to customers.

Optional assessment: 5 x 2 marks = 10 marks

Hidden depths [Creative comprehension – responding personally, higher-order-thinking skills, making links]

1 How persuasive is the visual and written text of this advertisement? Justify your opinion and give examples.
2 Who would be the target audience for this advertisement and where might you expect to see the advertisement?

Optional assessment: 2 x 2 marks = 4 marks

Extend yourself [Links to real life or other literature, researching, writing, creating, speaking tasks]

- Create your own advertisement for these products.
- Investigate the cost of these and other acne treatments and present your information in a table.
- Investigate recommended medical treatment for acne. Are such products necessary and effective?
- Look up the website and discuss with a partner its effectiveness and any new information gained.
- Create a TV or radio advertisement for an imaginary product, using persuasive language.

UNIT 20 Energy and the world

TEXT TYPE Argument
PURPOSE To persuade by putting forward an argument or particular point of view
STRUCTURE
1 Point of view is stated
2 Justifications of argument in a logical order
3 Summing up of argument

FEATURES Includes facts and figures, logical reasoning, examples, persuasive or emotive language

The quest for clean energy

Research into how we are to meet the world's growing energy needs without increasing global warming must begin now. Fifty years from now the planet will need three times the amount of energy now generated by using coal, oil and other fossil fuels.

The use of fossil fuels will need to be reduced dramatically, as they generate heat-trapping greenhouse gases which increase global warming.

Scientists have warned us the research effort needs to be equivalent to the Apollo project to put man on the moon. The Apollo project fulfilled President Kennedy's promise to put a man on the moon within 10 years. Millions of dollars were poured into this project during the 1960s, which accelerated the development of technology by decades. Just think of how different the world would be today if this mammoth effort hadn't been made.

According to a current research team of 18 scientists from academic, government and private research centres, many options need to be explored. Improving existing technologies and developing others such as fusion reactors or space-based solar power plants are suggestions they have made. Scientists say most energy technologies currently in existence either require research and development or are simply inadequate.

This assessment contrasts with the analysis made last year by the Intergovernmental Project on Climate Change, an international panel working under the United Nations. That analysis concluded that existing technologies such as solar panels, new nuclear power options, windmills, and filters for fossil fuel emissions would be climate-friendly and solve most of the problem.

Dr Haroon S. Kheshgi, a chemical engineer for Exxon Mobile, is one author of the new analysis. He said that 'climate change is a serious risk' and requires a shift away from fossil fuels. 'You need a quantum jump in technology,' he said. 'What we're talking about here is a 50 to 100 year time scale.'

The work needs to begin. There are few signs, however, that major industrial nations are prepared to support the quest for clean energy.

Europe and Japan have signed a climate treaty, the Kyoto Protocol, which involves meeting deadlines for cuts in gas emissions. Many leaders, in particular President Bush, have so far resisted any shift in energy policy. Leaders of some developing countries have rejected proposed cuts on their fast-growing use of fossil fuels. The countries which consume the most energy are industrialised countries. They consume 80 per cent of the world's energy, yet make up only 25 per cent of the world's population.

Leaders of developing countries believe the rich countries should act first.

Western, industrialised countries need to make research into climate-friendly energy a priority. Money needs to be poured into projects to find climate-friendly, sustainable energy sources. The future of the world's environment is at stake!

On the surface [Literal comprehension – right-there questions]

1 In 50 years' time how much energy will the world need?
2 How is energy generated now?
3 What do these fossil fuels generate?
4 If we continue to use fossil fuels, scientists are concerned about the increase in what?
5 What do the scientific researchers believe needs to be explored?

Optional assessment: 5 x 1 mark = 5 marks

Discovering techniques [Language structures and features, spelling, grammar, vocabulary]

1 Look up the following words in a dictionary and write out their meanings. Remember to keep in context with the passage.
a quest b consume c developing d industrialised
2 Connotations are the extra meaning we imply when we use words. For example, the word 'pollution' has negative connotations of our natural environment being poisoned by factories. What are the connotations of the word 'clean' in this text?
3 The shaded box at the top of the previous page lists the features commonly found in this style of writing. Find TWO examples of each (facts and figures/logical reasoning/examples/persuasive or emotive language) of these from the text.

Optional assessment: 3 x 2 marks = 6 marks

Search and think [Inferential and interpretive comprehension]

1 What does the new analysis by this group of scientists contrast with?
2 Which project in the 1960s was so well funded it advanced technological research by decades?
3 Are the existing technologies going to be adequate? Explain.
4 If research funding is not increased, how long will it take to research new technology for climate-friendly energy?
5 Why do you think the developing countries believe that the rich countries should act first?

Optional assessment: 5 x 1 mark = 5 marks

Hidden depths [Creative comprehension – responding personally, higher-order-thinking skills, making links]

1 Why do you believe leaders in developing countries will not cut back until rich countries do?
2 Do you get the impression as much money has been put into energy technology research as into the Apollo project? Add your own comment.

Optional assessment: 2 x 2 marks = 4 marks

Extend yourself [Links to real life or other literature, researching, writing, creating, speaking tasks]

- Find out what the current situation is with the Kyoto Protocol.
- Find out about the space-based solar panels that might beam energy to Earth using microwaves. Show in a diagram how this is done.
- Find out about new fusion-based power plants.
- Write a letter to Parliament giving reasons why New Zealand should/shouldn't have signed the Kyoto Protocol.

UNIT 21 Heads you win

TEXT TYPE Procedure/Instructions
PURPOSE To give instructions or show how something is accomplished through a series of steps
STRUCTURE
1 Opening statement of goal or aim
2 Materials required listed in order of use
3 Series of steps listed in order

FEATURES Logical sequence of steps, may use technical language and diagrams

Two-up

Players: any number can play
Age: mainly adults
Equipment: two coins and a flat piece of wood for throwing. Historically played with two pennies. The piece of wood was called a kip.

Two-up was an illegal gambling game for many years. The game was played almost anywhere by groups of men (known in those days as 'schools'). It was very common for the police to raid the well-known schools.

Today you will find two-up in games and souvenir shops. Two-up is sold in souvenir sets of old pennies and a wooden kip.

The professional game of two-up was controlled by a 'boxer' who was in charge of the betting and the spinning of the pennies.

The person who spun the coins was known as the spinner. The spinner bets on his or her ability to throw heads, and the other players in the game cover (or bet on) that player.

Spectators would wager side bets either for or against the spinner. The boxer collected a percentage, called a rake-off, from all the bets made, win or lose.

How to play

1 The spinner places two pennies on the flat piece of wood, known as the kip. When all bets have been placed the boxer notifies the spinner to begin by calling 'Come in, spinner.' The spinner throws the coins.
2 If the pennies are both heads up the spinner has won. He loses if they are both tails. If the pennies show one head, one tail then the throw is declared a no-throw and the spinner repeats the throw.
3 The spinner keeps throwing if heads come up. Heads must turn up three times before the spinner can take the winnings. This player can choose to play again or retire and the next spinner will step in.
4 If playing this at home, you can score how many times each player wins a round. This may be the best out of three or five rounds.

On the surface [Literal comprehension – right-there questions]

1 How many people can play the game of two-up at the same time?
2 List the equipment needed.
3 Where can you find two-up sets today?
4 What was the 'boxer' in charge of?
5 What did the 'boxer' collect?

Optional assessment: 5 x 1 mark = 5 marks

Discovering techniques [Language structures and features, spelling, grammar, vocabulary]

1 Make a list of the terms used in the game of two-up. Write your own definitions for the meanings of these words e.g. rake-off, boxer.
2 Why are instructions often provided in a numbered list?

Optional assessment: 2 x 2 marks = 4 marks

Search and think [Inferential and interpretive comprehension]

1 Explain the role of the spinner.
2 Who do the other players 'cover'?
3 Who do spectators wager their bets on?
4 What needs to happen for the spinner to win?
5 How can the scoring be done at home?

Optional assessment: 5 x 1 mark = 5 marks

Hidden depths [Creative comprehension – responding personally, higher-order-thinking skills, making links]

1 Which role would you most like to play in this game? Explain.
2 List as many games as you can think of that are similar to two-up. They need to involve chance or probability.

Optional assessment: 2 x 2 marks = 4 marks

Extend yourself [Links to real life or other literature, researching, writing, creating, speaking tasks]

- Find out more about the history of two-up and write a brief report on your findings.
- Play a game of two-up with some friends.
- Present a demonstration to the class on how to play the game. Then play a few rounds.
- Conduct some research about gambling. Write a report on your findings.
- Gambling is an issue in society. Write an argumentative essay for or against gambling being legalised.

UNIT 22

Animal rights

TEXT TYPE Discussion
PURPOSE To inform and persuade by presenting evidence and opinions about more than one side of an issue
STRUCTURE
1 Opening statement presenting the issue
2 Arguments or evidence for different points of view
3 Concluding recommendation
FEATURES Facts and figures, logical reasoning, examples, persuasive or emotive language

Equal rights for animals?

Human rights are also about human responsibilities to support freedom, justice and peace in the world. Do animals also have a 'right' to be treated in certain ways? The concept of rights is about shared responsibilities. We have a responsibility to animals, but do they have a responsibility to us?

Most animal welfare groups work from the assumption that animals deserve protection only when no serious human interests are at stake. If we were to keep dogs the way pigs are kept, we would be charged. People would find it unacceptable to keep a dog permanently in a narrow crate, tied at the neck so it can't turn around. Yet this treatment of pigs is justified because pigs provide pork, bacon and ham.

Professor Peter Singer, former professor of Philosophy at Monash University, whose book *Animal Liberation* became a landmark text, poses the question: If possessing a higher degree of intelligence does not entitle one human being to use another for its own ends, how can it entitle human beings to exploit non-human beings?

He argues that animals have the right to have their fundamental needs fulfilled, which are not the same needs as human beings.

Animal rights activists protest about the plight of battery hens, which are kept in cramped cages and 'debeaked'. They believe the treatment of these birds is cruel and that they should be allowed to roam free. Farmers argue that only healthy animals can provide us with healthy food. Both farmers and vets point out that diseases are common in all animals, regardless of whether they have been caged or not. Some diseases are made worse by intensive rearing. However, free-range living for chickens is not necessarily the answer. Most outbreaks of salmonella, which can lead to serious food poisoning, have occurred in the eggs of free-range, not battery-reared hens.

The issue is not simple. I believe we do have a moral duty towards animals; but given our biological position, what is that duty?

On the surface [Literal comprehension – right-there questions]

1 According to the article, what responsibilities do we have to other human beings?
2 What is the concept of 'rights' about?
3 What assumption do many animal welfare groups work from?
4 What does Professor Singer argue animals have a right to?
5 Outline the negatives for both free-range living and intensive rearing for chickens.

Optional assessment: 5 x 1 mark = 5 marks

Discovering techniques [Language structures and features, spelling, grammar, vocabulary]

1 Look up the following words in a dictionary and write out their meanings. Remember to keep in context with the passage.
   a responsibility   b right/s   c justified
   d exploit   e fundamental
2 List the evidence (facts and experts) used in this piece.

Optional assessment: 2 x 3 marks = 6 marks

Search and think [Inferential and interpretive comprehension]

1 Why are pigs treated differently to dogs?
2 True or false: Higher intelligence doesn't entitle one human being to use another.
3 What duty do we have to animals?
   a To not exploit them.
   b To be responsible for them.
4 Debeaking is not necessary for free-range chickens because:
   a they aren't kept in cramped spaces.
   b it's healthy.
5 What advantages does intensive rearing give to farmers?

Optional assessment: 5 x 1 mark = 5 marks

Hidden depths [Creative comprehension – responding personally, higher-order-thinking skills, making links]

1 Do you believe we have a moral duty to treat all animals equally?
2 How can we, as consumers, influence how farmers treat their livestock?

Optional assessment: 2 x 2 marks = 4 marks

Extend yourself [Links to real life or other literature, researching, writing, creating, speaking tasks]

- In the library, research battery hens. Present a brief report on your findings.
- What rights do animals have? Find out what animal liberationists believe are animal rights. Discuss your opinions in small groups.

UNIT 23

Read all about it

TEXT TYPE Cartoon
PURPOSE To entertain and/or make a social comment
STRUCTURE 1 Image or series of images usually in the form of line drawings
2 Written or spoken language accompanying images
FEATURES Visual and language cues to convey meanings at multiple levels; may be related to current affairs or issues

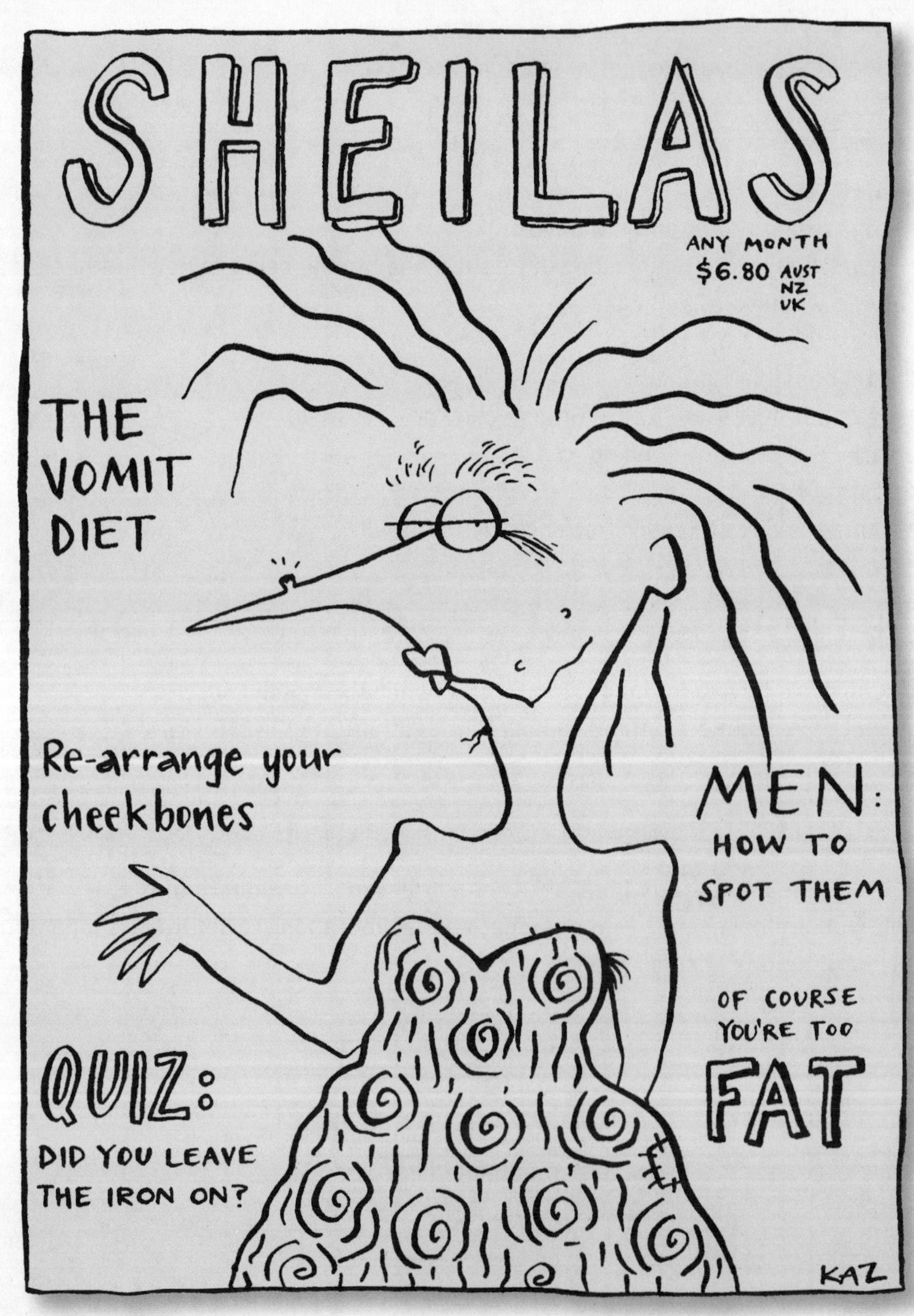

On the surface [Literal comprehension – right-there questions]

1 In which countries is *Sheilas* magazine available?
2 Is the magazine published weekly or monthly?
3 What is the name of the quiz in this edition?
4 Make a list of the beauty 'problems' that the character on the front page has.
5 What does the magazine advocate re-arranging?

Optional assessment: 5 x 1 mark = 5 marks

Discovering techniques [Language structures and features, spelling, grammar, vocabulary]

1 Write a definition of what is meant by the term 'body image'.
2 List three ways that a cartoon can be more powerful than text.

Optional assessment: 2 x 2 marks = 4 marks

Search and think [Inferential and interpretive comprehension]

1 List the articles that deal with body image.
2 What do you think the artist means by dating the magazine 'any month'?
3 What comment do you think the artist is making about articles such as 'Did you leave the iron on?' ?
4 According to *Sheilas* magazine, what are women/girls interested in?

Optional assessment: 4 x 1 mark = 5 marks

Hidden depths [Creative comprehension – responding personally, higher-order-thinking skills, making links]

1 This cartoon is making a comment about how the media promote a beauty myth and, therefore, create poor body image among women/girls. What are your thoughts on this issue?
2 Review the list of articles for *Sheilas* magazine. What topics do you think would be interesting for a women's/girls' magazine? Make a list.
3 Write a 300-word formal essay on body image. Focus on what you believe influences people in how they view themselves. What role do family and friends play in regard to self-image? Are the images portrayed in the media realistic and achievable? Remember to use the appropriate structure and conventions of formal essay writing.

Optional assessment: 3 x 2 marks = 6 marks

Extend yourself [Links to real life or other literature, researching, writing, creating, speaking tasks]

- Complete a survey of a range of magazines, for both boys/men and women/girls. Use the headings below to create a table for your findings

Title	Topics for articles	Image promoted	Products promoted

- Write a 500-word essay on body image. Focus on what you believe influences people in how they view themselves. What role do family and friends play in regard to self-image? Are the images portrayed in the media realistic and achievable?
- Make a list of your most positive qualities. The list may contain comments you have heard from other people as well as your own opinion. Include personal qualities as well as physical, e.g. good sense of humour, beautiful smile.
- Bulimia: write a brief report on this eating disorder.

UNIT 24 Chocaholics

TEXT TYPE Newspaper article
PURPOSE To persuade by putting forward an argument or particular point of view
STRUCTURE 1 Point of view stated
2 Justifications of argument in a logical order
3 Summing up of argument
FEATURES Facts and figures, logical reasoning, examples, persuasive or emotive language

Boutique industry creams the crop as chocaholics flock

BRUSSELS, Belgium • by Philip Buchanan

On a nondescript residential side street in this historic capital, the chocolate boutique Passion Chocolat has just opened its door at the genteel hour of midday. Within the first few minutes, nearly a dozen people crowd into the cosy confectionary to get their fresh fix. Seventy artfully displayed varieties, all meticulously handmade and no more than 5 days old, glisten in a glass case.

Rows of decadent, dark-chocolate squares. Silky-smooth milky mounds. Luscious ganaches. Tantalizing truffles. And the Bonaparte of Belgian bonbons: nutty pralines. Each one is an adventure in taste and a sensuous experience.

With a white cotton-gloved hand, the shop's petite owner, Claire Macq, gingerly boxes, wraps and beribbons the precious cargo, in a daily ritual repeated countless times in chocolate shops all across town.

Indeed, nowhere else is chocolate as celebrated as in Belgium, where it's comparable in status to wine in France or caviar in Russia. While its residents may be behind Switzerland and the United Kingdom in per capita consumption of the confection, Belgium (a nation of 10 million) boasts more than 2,100 chocolate shops. Brussels alone, with a population of just 1 million lists nearly 200 chocolate shops in the telephone directory. Moreover Belgium supports 290 chocolate-makers, 140 of which have fewer than five employees.

Many chocolatiers still make their praline by hand. They are mostly family businesses that have kept their methods and recipes as ferociously guarded as state secrets. Because each chocolatier has spent generations perfecting his own methods, there is great variety from one house to another. Here chocolate makers are more Willy Wonka than high-volume Hershey.

Passion Chocolat is the prime example of such small-scale operations. Claire Macq nearly emigrated to Australia after her first husband died but decided to open the business instead. Though the chocolates cost 45 Euro ($89) a kilo, customers are often queuing outside the shop by the time it opens. Across town in Rue Royale, Mary chocolates are also handmade, preservative-free and cost 48 Euro a kilo.

Different chocolatiers specialize in specific fillings, such as manon, filled with cream or butter and often coffee flavoured; gianduja, a paste made from mixing ground hazelnuts or grilled almonds with white sugar and cocoa butter or chocolate; or praline, a mixture based on roasted almond or hazelnuts, with cocoa butter or chocolate.

And the purchase of fine chocolate is not done casually. The shops themselves are places of elegance and refinement, and the customers are very knowledgeable, carefully picking and choosing, one by one, their assortment of the day.

Belgium's love affair with chocolate dates from 1857 when Jean Neuhaus left his native Switzerland to set up shop in Brussels. His grandson created the first filled chocolate. Chocolate-making really took off in the late 19th century, aided by Belgium's acquisition of the Congo and access to African cocoa fields.

But perhaps more important than history is the Belgian national obsession with chocolate. 'For us, chocolate is a devouring passion, a sweet addiction, and our nation's pride," writes Belgian Ruth Van Waerebeek in *Everybody Eats Well in Belgium Cookbook*. "Daily social life in Belgium would be unimaginable without chocolate."

Belgians rarely visit friends or relatives without bearing a beautifully adorned box. And just try to get a cup of restaurant coffee or tea without a requisite mini-square on the side.

Saying that Belgians love chocolate is a real understatement; for them chocolate is a devouring passion, a sweet addiction, and an essential part of their national pride.

On the surface [Literal comprehension – right-there questions]

1 Who wrote the article?
2 What time does Passion Chocolat open for business?
3 How many chocolate shops could you find in Belgium?
4 What is 'gianduja'?
5 When and why did chocolate making really take off?

Optional assessment: 5 x 1 mark = 5 marks

Discovering techniques [Language structures and features, spelling, grammar, vocabulary]

1 Use a dictionary to find the meanings of the following words. Remember to keep in context with the passage.
a nondescript b boutique c genteel d praline
e ritual f obsession g adorn(ed) h requisite
2 List the adjectives the author uses in the first three paragraphs.
3 Identify the metaphor from the following paragraph.
"With a white cotton-gloved hand, the shop's petite owner, Claire Macq, gingerly boxes, wraps and be-ribbons the *precious cargo*, in a daily ritual repeated countless times in chocolate shops all across town."
4 What language features can be found in the headline?

Optional assessment: 4 x 2 marks = 8 marks

Search and think [Inferential and interpretive comprehension]

1 Why do you think Claire Marq would wear a white cotton glove while packing customers' orders?
2 According to this article what do Belgian chocolate, French wine and Russian caviar have in common?
3 What is meant by the term 'small-scale operations'?
4 Clearly explain what the following sentence means: 'Here chocolate makers are more Willy Wonka than high-volume Hershey.'
5 Explain, using your own words, what is meant when the author says 'the purchase of fine chocolate is not done casually'?

Optional assessment: 5 x 1 mark = 5 marks

Hidden depths [Creative comprehension – responding personally, higher-order-thinking skills, making links]

1 One of the Belgian chocolate companies is called 'Passion Chocolat'. Look up 'passion' in the dictionary and copy the definition. Do you think it makes a good name for a chocolatier? Give reasons for your answer.
2 Write a paragraph describing the first time you tasted a handmade Belgian chocolate. (You might need to use your imagination!) Try to incorporate all the senses.

Optional assessment: 2 x 2 marks = 4 marks

Extend yourself [Links to real life or other literature, researching, writing, creating, speaking tasks]

- Design your own collection of special chocolates. Think carefully of which fillings you would choose and what each would look like. Write a description of your collection that would make a chocolate lover drool at the thought of eating it!
- Design a poster that advertises Passion Chocolat.
- Research the history of Cadbury NZ.

UNIT 25

Pop psychology

TEXT TYPE Magazine article (Quiz)
PURPOSE To entertain and inform
STRUCTURE
1 Orientation – background information about who, where and when
2 Series of events in chronological order
3 A personal comment
FEATURES Past tense, action verbs, descriptive language, may include quotes

The true you

from *Dolly* magazine

Think you know yourself pretty well? Follow the trail of questions to discover more about who you really are.

1 You wake up in the morning and throw on your favourite top. The colour of the top is:
a red **e** green
b baby pink **f** blue
c orange **g** purple
d yellow **h** white.

2 You close the gate behind you and head off. You'll be:
a jogging most of the way
b walking briskly
c strolling.

3 You've got a small backpack with you. You carry the back pack:
a on both shoulders
b slung over one shoulder.

4 You walk towards your fave spot near the water. The water is:
a the crashing surf of an ocean beach
b a flowing river, bubbling over rocks and pebbles
c a still lake, surrounded by sloping banks of reeds.

5 You notice a bridge you've never seen before. You:
a wonder where it leads, but carry on your way
b divert from your route, and follow the bridge to wherever it goes
c walk over for a look, but carry on your set path.

6 You make yourself comfortable next to a particular tree. The tree is:
a a tall, leafy tree with branches that spread high into the sky
b a weeping willow with long limbs trailing on the grass
c a low shrub with large leaves and pretty white flowers.

7 Sitting down to relax with a book, you choose to:
a lie on your back with your head resting on a grassy tuft
b sit up, leaning back with your legs in front and bent
c sit cross-legged and straight-backed.

8 While sitting near the water you see your favourite animal. List three things you love about this animal:

____

9 Near the water is a beautiful house. It's:
a on top of a grassy hill with no fence and a view of the water
b tucked into a sheltered hillside, with a large garden leading to the water
c nestled in a section of forest surrounded by a fenced garden.

10 At the front of the house is a fountain. You see its shape as:
a circular
b square or diamond.

11 As you approach the house, a person appears at the front door. You decide to:
a quickly turn and walk away, hoping they don't see you
b signal or wave, and approach them to explain that you're just looking at the fountain.

12 You decide to head home. There are two routes – via the road, which is quicker, or along the water, the way you came. Which one do you take?
a the longer route – you're in no rush
b the shorter route – there's no point in dawdling when you can go directly home.

(See page 74 for how well you scored.)

On the surface [Literal comprehension – right-there questions]

1 The quiz is based on a journey. List the activities you undertake on the journey.
2 Which question gives you the most range of choices?
3 Which question involves making a decision that may lead you off your path?
4 Which question asks you to imagine a house?
5 Where do you make yourself comfortable?

Optional assessment: 5 x 1 mark = 5 marks

Discovering techniques [Language structures and features, spelling, grammar, vocabulary]

1 Look up the following words in a dictionary and write out their meanings. Remember to keep in context with the passage.
   a extrovert b ambitious c sympathetic
   d vital e aspiring f spontaneous
2 The quiz focuses on the positive. Read the interpretation (12 a and b on page 74) for Question 12 of the quiz, 'The route home'. Rewrite it, focusing on the negative.

Optional assessment: 2 x 3 marks = 6 marks

Search and think [Inferential and interpretive comprehension]

1 What do you think the colours in Question 1 symbolise?
2 How did you decide when more than one option was appropriate?
3 In Question 3, how you wore the backpack relates to how others see you. What do you think each of the options suggests?
4 Question 2 deals with your approach to goals in life. Explain how your approach would vary depending on the activity.
5 What do bridges symbolise (Question 5)?

Optional assessment: 5 x 1 mark = 5 marks

Hidden depths [Creative comprehension – responding personally, higher-order-thinking skills, making links]

1 Did you enjoy the activity? Does the text fulfil the purpose of entertainment? Comment on what you learnt about yourself.
2 How realistic is this sort of quiz? Should it be taken seriously, or is it just for fun?

Optional assessment: 2 x 2 marks = 4 marks

Extend yourself [Links to real life or other literature, researching, writing, creating, speaking tasks]

- Make a poster/booklet entitled 'The true me'. Include things that show people what you are really like. You might like to include a picture of your favourite spot, your favourite animal or a house you love. You might talk about your favourite pastime, music, subject at school or fashion you are interested in. The list is endless so be creative.
- Research other magazine quizzes and note what topics they cover. Which type of quiz do you like most/least? Why?

UNIT 26 Working all day

TEXT TYPE Timetable
PURPOSE To display information about time, place and other relevant information efficiently
STRUCTURE Table format using words and numbers
FEATURES Abbreviations, technical language

School Timetable

TIMETABLE MONDAY	9.00–9.50	9.50–10.40	11.00–11.50	11.50–12.40	1.30–2.20	2.20–3.10
	PERIOD 1	**PERIOD 2**	**PERIOD 3**	**PERIOD 4**	**PERIOD 5**	**PERIOD 6**
7A	SOSE JSI A1	ENG JHU C4	MUSIC KDA H4	SCI TST B4	SPORT TNE	SPORT TNE
7B	SCI PDA B2	MATH CMA D1	ENG CSM C7	MUSIC KDA H4	SPORT SDA	SPORT SDA
7C	ITAL JBE C1	ENG JHE C1	SCI PDA B1	SOSE BDO D7	SPORT PWI	SPORT PWI
7D	ART KSI H2	ART KSI H2	ENG JHU C4	SOSE KRO A2	SPORT JDU	SPORT JDU
8A	MATH PWI D3	HEALTH TNE D6	ENG JHE D9	ENG JHE D9	ART KSI H2	ART KSI H2
8B	PE SDA GYM	PE SDA GYM	MATH JDU D3	ENG JHU C4	ART TCA H1	ART TCA H1
8C	HEALTH TNE D6	SOSE JSI D6	DRAMA KST H4	DRAMA KST H4	ENG CSM D7	ENG CSM D7
8D	ENG JHU C4	SOSE BDO C4	PE SDA GYM	PE SDA GYM	SCI PDA B1	SCI PDA B1
9A	SOSE BDO D7	ENG CSM D7	SCI TST B4	SCI TST B4	MUSIC KDA H4	MUSIC KDA H4
9B	ENG JHE D9	SOSE KRO A2	MATH CMA D1	ITAL JBE C1	DRAMA KST H3	DRAMA KST H3
9C	ART TCA H1	ART TCA H1	ENG JSM C4	SOSE JSI A2	SCI JDA B3	SCI JDA B3
9D	ENG CSM D2	MATH JDA D5	SCI JDA B3	SCI JDA B3 GYM	DRAMA TNE GYM	DRAMA TNE GYM
10A	MATH JDU D5	SCI JDU B3	ITAL TST C2	ITAL TST C2	ENVIRO KME A3	ENVIRO KME A3
10B	SCI JDA B3	SCI JDA B3	SOSE BDO D7	ENG JSM C4	FOODS KBE D10	FOOD KBE D10
10C	SCI TST B4	SCI TST B4	ITAL JBE C1	ENG CSM C7	PHOTO SST C10	PHOTO SST C10
10D	MATH CMA D1	ITAL TST C2	DRAMA TNE H3	DRAMA TNE H3	AUTO CWA T1	AUTO CWA T1
STAFF Drama & music	TNE – Terry Newton	KST – Kim Street	KDA – Karen Darma	**Foods**	KBE – Kris Belmore	
SOSE	JSI – Jim Smith	BDO – Betty Doyle	KRO – Karen Royland	**Environmental Studies**	KME – Kim Melwood	
Science	PDA – Paul Dalton	JDA – Jeff Dalgetty	TST – Tim Stevenson	**Photography**	SST – Stacey Stavrou	
Maths	PWI – Penny Wilmont	JDU – James Dupont	CMA – Con Martsakos	**Auto**	CWA – Charles Wallace	
ITC	JBE – Jane Bertolucci	TST – Trish Stamos	**Health & PE**	TNE – Ted Newby	SDA – Steve Dalgetty	
English	JHU – Jenny Huff	JHE – Jamie Heffernan	CSM – Carl Smith	JSM – Julie Smith		
Art	KSI – Kylie Simpson	TCA – Tristan Carnegie				
		INTERVAL	10.40–11.00	**LUNCH**	12.40–1.30	

On the surface [Literal comprehension – right-there questions]

1 How long do classes go for at this school?
2 List the initials for the three Drama/Music teachers.
3 On the timetable, in what order is the information presented?
   a Subject, teacher, room number
   b Teacher, subject, room number
   c Room number, teacher, subject
4 The classroom number also has the building block it is in before it. How many building blocks are there?
5 Which language other than English do students study at this school?
6 How many subjects only have one option of teacher?

Optional assessment: 6 x 1 mark = 6 marks

Discovering techniques [Language structures and features, spelling, grammar, vocabulary]

1 Abbreviations are a common feature of timetables. Why?
2 Acronyms are words made from the letters of other words. Look carefully at the acronyms created for the school's staff members. Can you work out how they have been made?

Optional assessment: 2 x 2 marks = 4 marks

Search and think [Inferential and interpretive comprehension]

1 On Monday, which subject does 8C have after interval until lunchtime?
2 Who does 8C have for Drama?
3 After lunch there are four classes not involved in sport or activity-based subjects. Which is the correct group of classes.
   a 8C, 8D, 9D, 10C
   b 8D, 8A, 9C, 10D
   c 8C, 8D, 9C, 10A
4 Drama is normally held in H3 and H4. 9D drama is in the Gym in the afternoon because:
   a there is more space.
   b the regular drama rooms have other classes in them.
5 How many breaks from class do the students get?

Optional assessment: 5 x 1 mark = 5 marks

Hidden depths [Creative comprehension – responding personally, higher-order-thinking skills, making links]

1 Generally speaking, academic subjects are done in the morning. Why do you think they are scheduled at this time?
2 In some countries, school begins at 8 a.m. and ends at 1 p.m. Students then go home, eat lunch and do their homework. What do you think of this approach?

Optional assessment: 2 x 2 marks = 4 marks

Extend yourself [Links to real life or other literature, researching, writing, creating, speaking tasks]

- Compare your school's timetable to the one on the previous page. How are the timetables similar? How are they different?
- Make up your own ideal timetable for one day.

UNIT 27 Going it alone

TEXT TYPE Narrative (Autobiography)
PURPOSE To tell a story
STRUCTURE
1 Orientation – who or what, where and when
2 Complication
3 Series of events
4 Resolution
FEATURES Use of past tense, pronouns

From *Lionheart* Jesse Martin (with Ed Gannon), *Lionheart: A Journey of the Human Spirit*

Sunday, December 7, 1998

With the genoa unfurled for the first time, I passed Sorrento, then Portsea, making my way through the South Channel to the starting line – the Heads of Port Phillip Bay, the most treacherous port entry and exit in the world.

I cut a thick slice of salami, then rushed up on deck to correct the wandering steering that had once again deviated slightly towards land. Maybe *Lionheart* was trying to tell me something. Maybe she'd prefer to stay at home in the shelter and safety of the bay rather than enter the unknown of Bass Strait. Did she know we were about to take on the world? Moments later I crossed the line, and my new life began.

What makes a seventeen-year-old decide to sail around the world? I'm not exactly sure, I was actually fourteen when I first started to think about doing so. When I sailed from Port Phillip Bay on 7 December, 1998, the trip was the culmination of years of dreaming.

Others may have thought I was a foolish young man, but I'd been working towards that dream for a long time.

Why? That's the question I get asked most. And one of the reasons behind this book. I don't just want to tell the story of how I sailed around the world on my own, but to reveal why a teenager would want to leave the comfort of home for eleven months at sea, and what I learnt from the experience.

It has been said that every great adventure begins with one small step. It's clichéd, but it's true. I've taken thousands of steps to become the youngest person to sail solo, non-stop and unassisted around the world.

But what was that first step? Was it sailing through the Port Phillip Heads, my official starting point of the trip? Was it waving goodbye to family and friends at the Sandringham Yacht Club? Was it when my major sponsor agreed to commit $160,000 to my trip? Was it that moment, at fourteen years of age, when I first dreamt of sailing around the world? Was it my previous adventures? Was it the first time I stepped aboard a boat? Was it when I was born?

Who knows, but I suspect Mum and Dad had a fair bit to do with it.

On the surface [Literal comprehension – right-there questions]

1 What has Jesse Martin achieved that makes him unique?
2 Which is the most treacherous port entry/exit in the world?
3 Who or what is *Lionheart*?
4 How old was Jesse Martin when he stared to think about sailing around the world?
5 What date did Jesse Martin set sail from Port Phillip Bay?
6 What does Jesse want to reveal in the book?

Optional assessment: 6 x 1 mark = 6 marks

Discovering techniques [Language structures and features, spelling, grammar, vocabulary]

1 What language feature is found in lines 6-9?
2 The 7th paragraph is made up entirely of what language feature?
3 Jargon is the use of special language by a group of people who deal with the same topic. List the examples of sailing jargon you can find in this extact.

Optional assessment: 3 x 2 marks = 6 marks

Search and think [Inferential and interpretive comprehension]

1 Jesse Martin says he's taken thousands of steps to become the youngest person to sail solo around the world. What do you think he means by the word 'thousands'?
2 Who do you think has been the biggest influence on Jesse in this adventure?
3 What is the significance of the name of Jesse's boat, *Lionheart*?
4 Which words indicate he was a bit anxious on his first part of the journey?
5 How did some people react to his plan to sail solo around the world?

Optional assessment: 5 x 1 mark = 5 marks

Hidden depths [Creative comprehension – responding personally, higher-order-thinking skills, making links]

1 How would you have felt sailing out through Port Phillip Heads that day? Write a diary entry explaining what you think your thoughts and feelings would have been.
2 Outline some of the dreams you have had (big or small). How many steps will you need to take to achieve them?

Optional assessment: 2 x 2 marks = 4 marks

Extend yourself [Links to real life or other literature, researching, writing, creating, speaking tasks]

- Read the rest of the Jesse Martin's book.
- Make a mind map of Jesse Martin's personal qualities.
- Most parents of a 17-year-old wouldn't allow him or her to sail around the world. Write a 500-word personal piece on how people's faith in you builds your confidence. Comment on your faith in your abilities, or comment on what you would like people to have faith in you about.
- It took great courage for Jesse's parents to allow him to go on this journey. Interview your own parents on the bravery it takes sometimes to be a parent, in allowing children to explore the world around them. Write a report on your findings, including a comment on what you have learnt from the interview.

UNIT 28

Jet careers

TEXT TYPE Interview transript
PURPOSE To get specific information directly from the person in question
To entertain and inform
STRUCTURE 1 A series of logically ordered, open questions
2 Answers from the interviewee
FEATURES Language may be formal or informal depending on purpose and audience

BANG ON

CHERYL SMITH HAS ALMOST COMPLETED HER JEWELRY MAKING APPRENTICESHIP. AT HER WELLINGTON WORKSHOP, THERE ARE SWEATY, MUSCLY MEN EVERYWHERE BUT THIS LONESOME FEMALE IS PROVING THAT GIRLS CAN DO ANY TRADE – INCLUDING ONE WITH HEAVY TOOLS.

WHERE DID YOU TRAIN?

I went to CIT and did a Design and Craft course but they didn't touch on jewellery. I didn't know how to get into it so I started a watchmaker's apprenticeship but I didn't like it at all. Then I found a course at MIT called Jewellery Techniques. That covered all sorts of things. It doesn't really get you ready for trade work. A lot of it was for craft jewellery but it does teach you that it's not all pretty, that it is hard work and you do need to be reasonably strong and driven. Out of 15 only 3 of us went on to do apprenticeships. I came home and worked in retail for a while and then got offered this apprenticeship.

HOW IS STUDY DIFFERENT FROM THE REAL WORLD?

Study doesn't prepare you for things like repairs. Repairs are huge in jewellery. You do so many repairs and alterations of other people's work. The course was aimed at you making stuff which was good if that's your thing. The tutor was very talented. But when you get into a shop and you need rings made smaller, we didn't learn that on the course. So you do need to do an apprenticeship and work with people who know what they're doing and are willing to train you.

HOW DID YOU GET IT?

I was working at Stewart Dawsons and my current employer knew me through that. They asked if I'd like to come work here.

WHY DIDN'T YOU COME IN HERE AND ASK FOR AN APPRENTICESHIP?

I didn't know how to do that. I'm very shy and didn't know how to push myself forward. I didn't know that I had to go knocking on doors. I asked at one jewellers and they didn't take apprentices. You either need to know people in business or need to be quite driven to push yourself forward.

ARE THERE MANY OPPORTUNITIES?

It's really hard to get into. It's not really aimed at females. You do have to be strong. The guys who work here all have quite big arms. It's physical work ... rollers and hammers and angles. Lots of forging.

DO YOU GO TO THE GYM?

Nah, I'm a big wimp. I've found a way to get around those things.

I THOUGHT JEWELLERY MAKING WAS FIDDLY AND DELICATE?

It is fiddly but the majority of jewellers are male. It's hard and it's dirty but it's very rewarding. These guys have been doing it for years.

WHAT'S YOUR DAILY GRIND LIKE?

I clean up, I set up shop and then the majority of my work is trade work which is like repairs. Also I am learning to do remakes and new rings but that's quite a small part, which is a shame.

WHAT'S THE APPRENTICESHIP LIKE?

You do apprentice papers though the open polytech, assignments and a final exam. So you work full time and study at night. I have six months to go!

THEN WHAT?

I hope they keep me. Just because you've finished your apprenticeship doesn't mean you've finished learning. There's ten years' worth of learning to do. I'm lucky here. They encourage us to make whatever we want. A lot of manufacturing jewellers are straight forward traditional. If you want to do more contemporary stuff it's best to be a craft jeweller. Here, we do everything. Each guy here has a different specialty.

BEST BITS?

Seeing your idea come out in front of you. When a job goes well and someone says 'Wow, I love this', it feels really good. It's very satisfying to know that someone's going to wear it for ever.

WORST BITS?

When the job's not working. It's hard work physically. It's hot and you get frustrated as you're working with little things all the time. Things don't necessarily go to plan all the time. What you think is a straightforward ring is actually someone's great-grandmother's precious ring with 20 years of repairs done to it. You touch it and it falls apart so it's up to you to fix it.

SO IF SOMEONE WANTS TO BECOME A JEWELLER, WHAT SHOULD THEY DO?

I would suggest looking for an apprenticeship straight away. Go door to door. If you want to be a jeweller you need to be a person who is good with your hands, you need to be able to get out there and knock on some doors.

WHAT'S YOUR DREAM?

I want my own gallery. I will have work that isn't just jewelry. Jewelry, art and sculpture.

On the surface [Literal comprehension – right-there questions]

1 What formal training has Cheryl Smith completed?
2 How many students from her MIT class went on to do apprenticeships?
3 Are most jewellers male or are they female?
4 What does the majority of Cheryl's day-to-day work involve?
5 What is Cheryl's long-term dream?

Optional assessment: 5 x 1 mark = 5 marks

Discovering techniques [Language structures and features, spelling, grammar, vocabulary]

1 Explain the pun in the title.
2 Even the media get it wrong sometimes! There is an inconsistency in the spelling of a significant word throughout this article. Identify the word and give a reason why this mistake could have been made.

Optional assessment: 2 x 2 marks = 4 marks

Search and think [Inferential and interpretive comprehension]

1 What did Cheryl not learn as part of her course?
2 Why is the jewellery industry so male dominated?
3 What does Cheryl find most satisfying about her job?
4 Write the question/heading that you think best gets Cheryl to talk about her immediate future.
5 What is the key personality trait that Cheryl thinks you need if you want to get a jewellery apprenticeship?

Optional assessment: 5 x 1 mark = 5 marks

Hidden depths [Creative comprehension – responding personally, higher-order-thinking skills, making links]

1 Does Cheryl make this career seem appealing? Why?/Why not?
2 It is good to have dreams for the future. What would your dream job be?

Optional assessment: 2 x 2 marks = 4 marks

Extend yourself [Links to real life or other literature, researching, writing, creating, speaking tasks]

- What else would you like to know about jewellery making? Write five more questions you would like to ask Cheryl.
- Research a career that interests you and write it up as though you have carried out an interview. Attempt to copy the style of this text.
- Get a *Jet* magazine (sent free to your school each month) and read through the careers presented. Which one appeals the most? Why?

UNIT 29 Rating the movies

TEXT TYPE Response, film review
PURPOSE To review a text
STRUCTURE 1 Review
2 Context – background information on the text
3 Description of the text (including characters and plot)
4 Concluding statement (judgement, opinion or recommendation)
FEATURES Language may be formal or informal depending on purpose and audience, may include examples and quotes

Rabbit Proof Fence

FILMINK rates movies out of $13.50, the maximum price charged at cinemas. The FILMINK rating system indicates the amount we believe each ticket to the movie to be worth.

Witnessing the discovery and development of new cinematic talent can be a profoundly rich and rewarding experience. Brushing aside the old adage that you should never work with children, Australian director Phillip Noyce (hauling back to his homeland after taking on Hollywood with films like *Patriot Games*, *The Saint* and *The Bone Collector*) has had the [courage] to let his dazzling new film rest on the very small shoulders of three extraordinary young actresses. But it's more than just a film on their shoulders – it's also symbolically the weight of over 200 years of colonialism and political miscarriage. It's a tough burden, but their backs hold firm.

It's '30s Australia, and the initiation of what would later become termed The Stolen Generation is in full swing. Under the auspices of Mr A.O. Neville, The Chief Protector of Aborigines (a fine turn from Kenneth Branagh, who makes the character a complex figure, and never reduces him to a mere villain), Aboriginal children of 'mixed blood' are being torn from their families to be integrated into white Australian society, with the aim of ultimately 'bleeding out' the indigenous population. Molly, Daisy and Gracie (Everlyn Sampi, Tianna Sansbury, Laura Monaghan) are three such children, but they don't buckle under and conform – they escape the mission where they are being taught to work as domestics and flee across the desert, starting a 1500 mile journey to be reunited with their mother.

Filmed in tight, muscular style by action master Noyce – and shot through the expertly judged lens of Christopher Doyle (*In the Mood for Love*), who gives the Australian outback a look all its own – *Rabbit Proof Fence* powerfully blends political force with shattering human emotion. This largely comes conveyed through the incredible work of Everlyn Sampi, Tianna Sansbury and Laura Monaghan. With the raw, loose-limbed expression only found in non-actors, they're totally believable at every turn, and make *Rabbit Proof Fence* a film every bit as moving and unforgettable as it is socially relevant, and ultimately groundbreaking.

Rating: PG
Country: Australia
Cast: Everlyn Sampi, Tianna Sansbury, Laura Monaghan, Kenneth Branagh
Distributor: REP Worth: $12.00
Released: February 21 (nationally)
Time: 92 Minutes
Director: Phillip Noyce

Erin Free, *Rabbit Proof Fence*, *Filmink*, February 2002

On the surface [Literal comprehension – right-there questions]

1 What film is being reviewed here and who directed it?
2 Who wrote this film review?
3 Where was this review published?
4 List three factors that contributed to this film's success.
5 Who are the four main actors in this film?
6 What other films has Phillip Noyce directed?

Optional assessment: 6 x 1 mark = 6 marks

Discovering techniques [Language structures and features, spelling, grammar, vocabulary]

1 Who might be the intended audience for this film review? Provide support for your answer.
2 There is some difficult vocabulary in this text. Choose ten words you are unsure of the meaning of and look them up in a dictionary.
3 List the adjectives the writer uses to describe the film.

Optional assessment: 3 x 2 marks = 6 marks

Search and think [Inferential and interpretive comprehension]

1 What was challenging for Phillip Noyce about the main actors in this film?
2 It has been said that this film, *Rabbit Proof Fence*, has a purpose beyond providing entertainment. Explain what you think this means.
3 From the information in this review, who is 'The Stolen Generation'?
4 Does Kenneth Branagh play the part of Mr A.O. Neville effectively? Provide support for your answer.
5 How highly does the reviewer rate this film?

Optional assessment: 5 x 2 marks = 10 marks

Hidden depths [Creative comprehension – responding personally, higher-order-thinking skills, making links]

1 What is the purpose of most films? Is social relevance or commentary necessary for a film to be considered excellent? Discuss this issue, providing supporting evidence.

Optional assessment: 2 x 3 marks = 6 marks

Extend yourself [Links to real life or other literature, researching, writing, creating, speaking tasks]

- View the film *Rabbit Proof Fence*. What does the title mean and is it effective?
- Design a film poster for *Rabbit Proof Fence*.
- Collect film reviews and read them aloud as if for television presentation. Do written reviews need to be modified for this different mode of communication? What other cues could assist in a television review?
- Research films that have been nominated for or won best film Oscars. What trends can you discover in these selections?

UNIT 30 From the director

TEXT TYPE Recount
PURPOSE To reconstruct past experiences by retelling events
STRUCTURE 1 Background information about who, where and when
2 Series of events in chronological order
3 A personal comment (optional)
FEATURES Use of past tense, action verbs, descriptive language, may include quotes

Phillip Noyce – Rabbit Proof Fence director by Erin Free

Dead Calm

After making some of the biggest movies, and working with some of the biggest stars, in Hollywood, Australian Phillip Noyce returns home with *Rabbit Proof Fence*, a powerful film about Aboriginal Australia and the stolen generation. He spoke to *FILMINK*'s Erin Free about coming back from Hollywood, his new film and its relevance in today's political climate.

Film director Phillip Noyce is the calm at the eye of the storm. Currently in post-production on *The Quiet American* (starring Brendan Fraser and Michael Caine), and preparing for the major release of *Rabbit Proof Fence*, his first Australian-set film in many years, Noyce is surrounded by swirling activity. But all through it, he remains dead calm, whether he's talking on the phone about getting trailers for the film just right or dealing with his staff. Years in Hollywood working on big budget films … seem to have taught him the admirable skill of grace under fire. … 'It was a combination of things that happened in America and things that happened here,' the imposing Noyce explains in his Fox Studios office of his decision to return home. 'I was working on *The Sum of All Fears* with Harrison Ford. The problem was that Harrison was never sure that he wanted to do it … It just made me think of the machine that I found myself in – the Hollywood machine … I started to have doubts myself about the whole process that I was part of. … I'd been given the script for *Rabbit Proof Fence* many months before, and I'd met with the writer Christine Olsen and I'd explained that I didn't think I'd be able to do it. It was a wonderful story, and the time to make it was now, and not in three years' time when I became available. But I couldn't get the story out of my head … So I said to my producing partner that I should go to Australia and make that film, almost as an antidote to the nonsense that I was finding myself a part of in America. In Australia, I had a film budgeted at $5 million US with no stars and a story that was emotionally extremely compelling. So I caught a plane straight to Sydney.'

Dealing with the forced removal of three young Aboriginal girls from their family and their displacement to a government settlement where they'll be taught the ways of white Australia and how to work as domestic servants, Noyce says that *Rabbit Proof Fence* was a story of burning social relevance that needed to be told now. 'When you're a director and you're considering a project, you wet your finger and you test the wind, which I did for this film,' he explains. 'I was aware of the sea change that had taken place in Australia over the last ten years, with the change in attitude of white Australia to their history with black Australia. I was aware that there was a strong need to come to terms with a past that had been stolen from us. We couldn't remember it because there was so much that was hidden: we couldn't read about it or learn about it. But I got the sense that there was this want to come to terms with this past. When I think about this film, I don't think we've come up with a story, and then we're trying to sell it to the audience. I actually think the audience wants the vehicle that will help them come to terms with a deep, dark secret that they know is lurking in the cupboard. This was confirmed to me just a few weeks ago when we ran a competition as a result of screening a series of stories on *The Today Show*, where people had to tell us why they wanted to see the film. We got 1500 entries within a week, and they were incredibly revealing.'…

Dealing with essentially a cast of young non-actors and a much lower budget on *Rabbit Proof Fence* made for a refreshing change for Noyce, particularly with its lack of big movie stars. 'We were freed from the pressures of trying to deal with the star system, which is the most savage gauntlet that you can run in Hollywood.'… 'Hollywood is really run by the superstars: it's an industry set up for their convenience and profit. They're the ones who'll profit and not be inconvenienced whether the film loses $100 million or makes $100 million…'

With *Rabbit Proof Fence*, Phillip Noyce seems to have come full circle, finally returning to the country that inspired him to get into the film business in the first place. 'When I was a little kid growing up in Griffith, there were all sorts of shows that came to town, from Ma and Pa magic shows right through to The Worth Family Circus, who went from town to town on a train. It was all on a train, and I'd look into the windows, and that whole world fascinated me, the way they'd pull up stakes and go from town to town. And that's kind of what I've been doing ever since, taking these movie sets all around the world.'

On the surface [Literal comprehension – right-there questions]

1 What nationality is the director Phillip Noyce?
2 Where does Phillip Noyce usually work?
3 Where was the film *Rabbit Proof Fence* made?
4 How can we tell which words Phillip Noyce actually said in answer to the interviewer's questions?
5 What sort of shows did Phillip Noyce enjoy as a child growing up in Griffith?

Optional assessment: 5 x 1 mark = 5 marks

Discovering techniques [Language structures and features, spelling, grammar, vocabulary]

1 List the contractions (e.g. 'I'm') used in this text.
2 This interview includes several clichés or overused phrases. Explain the meaning of the following:
'the calm at the eye of the storm'
'the most savage gauntlet you can run'
'to have come full circle'.

Optional assessment: 2 x 2 marks = 4 marks

Search and think [Inferential and interpretive comprehension]

1 Why did Phillip Noyce think *Rabbit Proof Fence* needed to be made as soon as possible?
2 What evidence is given in this interview of public interest in the 'stolen generation'?
3 What major differences between the Hollywood and Australian film industries are highlighted in this interview?
4 How do you think Phillip Noyce feels about the Hollywood system and how might this cause conflicts for him in his work as a director?
5 Why did Philip Noyce run a competition on *The Today Show*?

Optional assessment: 5 x 2 marks = 10 marks

Hidden depths [Creative comprehension – responding personally, higher-order-thinking skills, making links]

1 Explain in your own words what Noyce meant when he said 'Hollywood is really run by the superstars'.
2 Consider movie themes that could emerge from current events in New Zealand and the world in the next few years. Make a list of possibilities.

Optional assessment: 2 x 3 marks = 6 marks

Extend yourself [Links to real life or other literature, researching, writing, creating, speaking tasks]

- Rewrite this magazine interview as a television interview, using a question-and-answer format. Then perform it for the class.
- Watch and read some interviews of the same personalities by different interviewers and make up a class list of criteria for what makes a great interviewer and interviewee.

UNIT 31 An unhappy customer

TEXT TYPE Letter of complaint

PURPOSE To communicate information, experiences or ideas, formally or informally, in writing to a reader who is not present

STRUCTURE
1. Address and date
2. Greeting or salutation
3. Series of events or issues in paragraphs
4. Sign off

FEATURES Set layout, informal or formal language depending on purpose and audience, varied sentences

14 Geoffrey Cres
Chatswood
North Shore City
Auckland

Jetsons Scooter Company

29 January 2007

Dear Mr Jetson,

I am writing to register a complaint about the quality of your motorised scooter MX5, and to inform you of the poor service I have received from your company. I purchased an MX5 from Wonder World Leisure Goods in Chatswood on 15 December for my son's Christmas present. James was so very pleased with this gift, as he had wanted one of your scooters for years. The scooter was well used for only a month when it broke down.

We returned the scooter to Wonder World who informed us that they took no responsibility for repairs on goods purchased at their shop. We were referred to your company. I rang the service section, and was told the scooter was not covered by warranty.

James was very upset, as he dearly wanted to use the scooter. I inquired about getting the motor repaired, assuming that your company would be able to do this or at least refer me to someone who could. I was told that Jetson Scooters have no obligation to repair goods or to refer people to repairers.

I then took the scooter to a lawnmower repairman, who informed me that the part that needed replacing was available only from your company. I then had to ring and ask for the part, which obviously wasn't very good quality if it needed repairing after only one month, and then return to the lawnmower repairman to fix the problem.

The repairs have cost me $50, the part $25; and needless to say we have been inconvenienced having to make phone calls and find alternatives for repairing the goods.

As a manufacturer of goods you should have some responsibility to your customers, not only to provide quality goods, but also to provide some sort of service in the event of their breaking down. I am not impressed with the quality of your goods or service and will certainly not be recommending others to buy your products.

Yours sincerely

S Mackay

Mr S Mackay

On the surface [Literal comprehension – right-there questions]

1 What is the complainant's name?
2 Whose scooter is it?
3 Which model of scooter is it?
4 Which company produced the scooter?
5 Who eventually repaired the scooter?

Optional assessment: 5 x 1 mark = 5 marks

Discovering techniques [Language structures and features, spelling, grammar, vocabulary]

1 Circle the phrases which might have been used in advertising this scooter. Then add some of your own words/phrases to the list.

four exciting new colours	great colours: red, green, orange
lightweight	about 3 kilograms
wham! and you're ready to scoot	takes about 2 minutes to set up
motorised	top-of-the-range motor

2 Write an advertisement for a company which offers follow-up service using the following words: quality, referral, recommendation.

Optional assessment: 2 x 3 marks = 6 marks

Search and think [Inferential and interpretive comprehension]

1 Was Mr S Mackay complaining because there was no warranty on the scooter?
2 What do you think Mr Mackay expected when he rang the service section of the company?
3 What does Mr Mackay believe the company's responsibility is?
4 What impression is he left with in regard to the attitude of the company to its customers?
5 What does Mr Mackay threaten to do?

Optional assessment: 5 x 1 mark = 5 marks

Hidden depths [Creative comprehension – responding personally, higher-order-thinking skills, making links]

1 Have you ever had faulty goods not covered by warranty? Explain what happened and how you felt. Would you buy goods without a warranty? Explain.
2 Do you believe manufacturers have a duty to their customers after purchase of goods? Explain why or why not. Give some specific examples.

Optional assessment: 2 x 2 marks = 4 marks

Extend yourself [Links to real life or other literature, researching, writing, creating, speaking tasks]

- Find out about the Consumers' Institute. Write a brief report on what they do and the service they provide.
- Find out about the Disputes Tribunal. What do they deal with? Write a brief report outlining their role in the legal system. Give a presentation to your class explaining the role of this body. Give examples of products they may need to go to the tribunal about.
- Find the warranties for three goods in your home. Outline what is covered by warranty and how long the warranty lasts for.
- Select one product that you own. Develop your own warranty statement. Make sure it is fair to both the manufacturer and the consumer.

UNIT 32 Tickle the taste buds

TEXT TYPE Menu
PURPOSE To display available food choices
STRUCTURE 1 List of courses in order of service
2 Details of dishes in each course outlined
FEATURES Technical language relating to ingredients and food preparation

Round-the-world dinner party

Hors-d'oeuvres: Asia
Vegetable rice paper rolls (Vietnam)
Samosas (India)
Spring rolls (China)
Sushi (Japan)

Entrée: Middle East
Hummus and eggplant dips with bread
Vines leaves, stuffed
Fried cheese

Main: Europe
Coq au Vin (France)
Beef Wellington (England)
Roast vegetables
Brussels sprouts, bacon, squash and cracked pepper

Dessert: USA
Pecan pie
Bombe Alaska
Cherry pie

On the surface [Literal comprehension – right-there questions]

1 How many courses are there on this menu?
2 List the countries where the hors-d'oeuvres come from.
3 Which course serves pies?
4 Which course serves a lot of vegetables?
5 Which course does not list countries, only the region?

Optional assessment: 5 x 1 mark = 5 marks

Discovering techniques [Language structures and features, spelling, grammar, vocabulary]

1 Find out the meanings of the following words: hors-d'oeuvres, entrée.
2 Find two other words from a language other than English used for referring to food or drinks in recipes.

Optional assessment: 2 x 2 marks = 4 marks

Search and think [Inferential and interpretive comprehension]

1 Which course is more likely to be served before guests move to the dinner table?
2 Which other course on the menu is likely to be shared with others?
3 Which direction around the world are we going?
4 Is the food on the menu from the northern or southern hemisphere?
5 If one of the guests were vegetarian, which dishes could they eat?

Optional assessment: 5 x 1 mark = 5 marks

Hidden depths [Creative comprehension – responding personally, higher-order-thinking skills, making links]

1 List the food on this menu you have not tried before. List the food that you would really like to eat. Which wouldn't you eat? Why?
2 The menu is very extensive. Which courses may be skipped? Explain.

Optional assessment: 2 x 2 marks = 4 marks

Extend yourself [Links to real life or other literature, researching, writing, creating, speaking tasks]

- The menu stops in the USA. Make up another dinner party menu of your own for the remainder of the journey. Include: Central America, South America, Africa, New Zealand and the Pacific. You will need to find out the sort of foods people typically eat in these areas.
- Write up a dinner menu for you and your friends with your favourite foods listed. Place in brackets the countries these dishes come from.
- Create a vegetarian or low-fat menu for your guests.
- Make a list of foods you know are traditionally eaten with your hands.
- Find out more about how food is served in certain cultures, i.e. in some cultures food is served in the centre of the table for everyone to share; in some cultures salad is served after the main course.
- Write a report on any interesting traditions, outlining the country or culture which follows this practice.

UNIT 33 Cooking for friends

TEXT TYPE	Instructions/Procedure
PURPOSE	To give instructions or show how something is accomplished through a series of steps
STRUCTURE	1 Opening statement of goal or aim 2 Material required listed in order of use 3 Series of steps listed in chronological order
FEATURES	Logical sequence of steps, may use technical language

Fried rice

Serves 4
Cooking time: 10 mins
Preparation time: 20 mins

2 eggs
3 tablespoons oil
1 onion (chopped)
1/4 cup bacon bits
260 g ham (chopped)
1/4 cup peas
1 1/3 cups cooked rice (store in fridge)
3 spring onions (chopped)
2 tablespoons soy sauce
270 g small prawns (cooked)

1. Lightly beat the two eggs. Pour 1 tablespoon of the oil into the wok and cook the eggs as an omelette. Take the omelette out and put aside.
2. Place 2 tablespoons of the oil in the wok and add the onion and bacon bits, stir until onion is transparent. Add ham and cook for another minute.
3. Add the peas (precooked or frozen) and rice. Stir-fry for 4 minutes. The rice should be heated all the way through and be slightly golden.
4. Cut the omelette into thin strips and add to the mixture. Add the chopped spring onion, soy sauce and the prawns. Cook for an additional minute. Serve.

On the surface [Literal comprehension – right-there questions]

1 Which ingredient needs to be precooked and stored in the fridge?
2 How long are the peas cooked for?
3 How many people does this recipe serve?
4 How many eggs are in the omelette?
5 How much preparation time is required?

Optional assessment: 5 x 1 mark = 5 marks

Discovering techniques [Language structures and features, spelling, grammar, vocabulary]

1 Find out what the following abbreviations in recipes stand for.
a °C b tsp c c d tbsp
2 Put the following in order from the smallest amount to the largest.
cup teaspoon pinch tablespoon dessertspoon 500 mL

Optional assessment: 2 x 2 marks = 4 marks

Search and think [Inferential and interpretive comprehension]

1 Does the preparation time include the time needed to cook and refrigerate the rice?
2 List the ingredients that need to be prepared before cooking. Which would you do first? Why?
3 Why do you think the omelette is included only at the end?
4 Which ingredients in this recipe would require further knowledge as to how to cook them?
5 Why do you think the onion and bacon bits are the first ingredients to be cooked in the wok?

Optional assessment: 5 x 1 mark = 5 marks

Hidden depths [Creative comprehension – responding personally, higher-order-thinking skills, making links]

1 Did you find the recipe easy to follow? Does it inspire you to cook this dish? Which foods do we tend to buy and not cook ourselves? Why?
2 You can add and take out parts of this recipe. What would you add to or take out from the ingredients to make your own version of fried rice? What else would you serve as an accompanying dish to fried rice?

Optional assessment: 2 x 2 marks = 4 marks

Extend yourself [Links to real life or other literature, researching, writing, creating, speaking tasks]

- Find alternative recipes in cookbooks and compare ingredients.
- Find out how long it takes to cook rice and the different ways you can do it.
- Do a cookery demonstration for your class, instructing them how to make fried rice.
- With a partner, prepare an oral presentation about dishes using rice from different countries. On a map show which countries use rice as a staple food.

UNIT 34

The root of all evil!

TEXT TYPE Speech
PURPOSE To persuade, inform, entertain
STRUCTURE 1 Opening statement – introduction to the subject
2 Justifications of argument in a logical order
3 Concluding statement – summing up of argument.
FEATURES Speech writing techniques: anecdotes, emotive words, examples, statistics, figures of speech, humour, personal pronouns, etc.
Delivery techniques: gesture, intonation, pause, visual aids, voice, facial expressions, intonation, etc.

Television. The root of all evil. Or at least that's what my parents would like you to believe! Whether it be watching the programmes free to air, checking out the latest DVD or whiling away an afternoon – so perhaps the majority of the day! – reaching the next level of an Xbox game, it is 'evil'. A time-wasting, brain-frying, square-eying evil.

But how many of you here would agree with my parents' opinion of the evil device sitting so innocently in the corner of the room? Not many I bet. In fact most of you could probably lay the blame of our current addiction to the box squarely at our parents' feet. How old were you when you were encouraged to give your parents some peace and quiet by sitting in front of the television watching *Bob the Builder*? Who bought the 42" wide-screen plasma positioned as the focal point of your lounge? Not to mention the smaller, cheaper version in the family room, the even smaller one in the guest room and for the lucky among us, our bedroom? I don't need to tell you the answer as I assume we are all on the same wavelength. But, oh, how those very same people complain at our 'couch potato' lifestyle. Well, the time has come for us to fight, if not for ourselves then for the future generations who risk losing one of teenagers' favourite pastimes!

In the next few minutes (basically the time length of the average ad break because apparently we teenagers can't concentrate because of the effect television has had on us!) I am going to present to you exactly why it is I see television as a fundamental in the education and social development of today's teenagers.

...

Let's move on to another aspect of television that parents like to rubbish – PlayStation (and/or Xbox). I am sure many of you have experienced the 'Monday to Friday Ban' or perhaps even the 'Total Shutdown'. Over the years the old-fashioned 'video game' has developed into a multimillion, perhaps even billion, dollar industry but the positive potential of these games has been largely ignored by parents and I feel it is my duty to teenagers everywhere to spread the 'good news' about this pastime.

The good news centres on the skills that such games can impart. It has been proven by researchers that these games improve hand-eye coordination, improve reflexes, and can expand a teenager's social life by having the opportunity to interact with other children through multiplayer games. They can also improve logical thinking and problem-solving skills.

I went online to see if I could find anything 'hard core' that might persuade my parents to lighten up a little and came up with this:

(PowerPoint) 'While parents often wonder why their children are playing computer games rather than mix outside with their friends, many researchers say computer games are the key to success in an information age and kids are actually learning. Findings suggest that people who play computer games make sharper soldiers, drivers and surgeons, because their reaction time and peripheral vision is better. People who play computer games take risks and react with ease in stressful situations.'

Henry Jenkins, Director of Comparative Media Studies, Massachusetts Institute of Technology.

The same article explained:

(PowerPoint) 'In a hunting society, kids learned bows and arrows. In an information society, playing games with resource management – where you need to process massive amounts of information to determine which is important and which you let slide – might be the right kind of play. Furthermore, computer games can teach ethics, money-handling skills, how to read text, and multiplayer games broaden a player's social life so anyone regardless of colour, religion or age can be a leader in their own right.'

Henry Jenkins, Director of Comparative Media Studies, Massachusetts Institute of Technology.

Man, with stuff this good our parents should be paying us to play these games!

On the surface [Literal comprehension – right-there questions]

1 In a maximum of two sentences, explain the key ideas of this speech.
2 Who is the intended audience of this speech and how do you know?
3 Other than himself and his peers, who does the student believe he needs to fight for?
4 What have parents largely ignored about games such as PlayStation and Xbox?
5 Where did the student go to look for evidence to support his argument?

Optional assessment: 5 x 1 mark = 5 marks

Discovering techniques [Language structures and features, spelling, grammar, vocabulary]

1 Find an example of the following speech-writing techniques:

Listing	Colloquial	Personal pronouns
Cliché	Rhetorical question	Metaphor/Personification

2 Copy out the first paragraph of the speech into the middle of your page. Using a different-coloured pen for each annotation where you would use the following presentation techniques if you were presenting the speech to your class:

Gesture	Expression and intonation	Pause for emphasis

Optional assessment: 2 x 6 marks = 12 marks

Search and think [Inferential and interpretive comprehension]

1 Who does the student blame for teenagers' addiction to television?
2 What do you think the 'Monday to Friday Ban' is?
3 Why would a multiplayer game encourage social interaction?
4 Why does the speech writer think that parents 'should be paying us to play these games'?
5 Why is it important to use evidence to back up your argument/opinion?
6 The words 'PowerPoint' come up before each of the Henry Jenkins quotations. This suggests that the student used a PowerPoint presentation as part of his speech delivery. Give two reasons why it would be a good idea to use the quotations in this way.

Optional assessment: 6 x 1 mark = 6 marks

Hidden depths [Creative comprehension – responding personally, higher-order-thinking skills, making links]

1 Produce a two-column grid. Use the headings 'Positive' and 'Negative' for each column.
   a Using the grid, list the reasons why the student (and Henry Jenkins) sees these games as positive.
   b For every positive idea that you found, can you come up with a negative? You might like to use the Internet to help you.
2 The middle of this speech is missing. Can you tell what would have been spoken about by reading the introduction? Brainstorm and then write a paragraph about one of the ideas that would logically fit into the middle speech.

Optional assessment: 2 x 6 marks = 12 marks

Extend yourself [Links to real life or other literature, researching, writing, creating, speaking tasks]

- Write a speech that agrees with the statement 'Television is the root of all evil'.
- Complete the speech (by writing the middle and conclusion) and present it to the class.
- As a group, complete (by writing the middle and conclusion) the speech and take a paragraph each to present to the class.

'The true you' quiz (p. 54)

Score

1 FAVOURITE-COLOURED TOP: How you see yourself
- **a** RED: you're extroverted, ambitious and enjoy being the centre of attention.
- **b** BABY PINK: you're sympathetic and soft, playful and cheeky – the boys love you!
- **c** ORANGE: you're practical, energetic, creative and like to take action.
- **d** YELLOW: you're interesting, stimulating, lively, vital and aspiring.
- **e** GREEN: you're an observer of life – very cautious and intellectual.
- **f** BLUE: you're creative, perceptive, sensitive, imaginative and analytical.
- **g** PURPLE: you have deep feelings and aspirations – you are also interested and intuitive.
- **h** WHITE: you're highly individual, optimistic, well-balanced and in search of a simple life.

2 YOUR SPEED: Your approach to goals in life
- **a** You're impatient to reach your goals and actively strive to meet them.
- **b** There's no hurry, you're slowly but surely achieving your goals.
- **c** You're not in any great rush to achieve; you savour the small pleasures in life.

3 THE RUCKSACK: How other people see you
- **a** You're practical, organised and efficient. You look to the future and like to prepare for life's obstacles.
- **b** You're spontaneous, lively and disorganised. You live in the moment and deal with obstacles as they arise.

4 THE BODY OF WATER: Your inner romantic self
- **a** You're passionate, dynamic and on a roller-coaster when in love. While you love deeply, passion easily turns to fury.
- **b** You're flirtatious, playful and thrive on the novelty and uncertainty of new love. Boys are drawn to you, but you sometimes play games with them.
- **c** You love to be romanced and treated with respect. Romantically you are gentle, yet deep, and you don't love lightly.

5 THE BRIDGE: How adventurous you are
- **a** You're cautious and slow to take action. You're rarely led astray.
- **b** You're known for your sense of adventure. As far as you're concerned, life is a melting pot of potential experiences and you're keen to net your fair share.
- **c** You're inquisitive, but don't like to take risks. You'll choose the road well travelled over the challenge of the unknown.

6 THE TREE: Your view of your personality
- **a** You're confident in yourself and feel secure about your place in the world.
- **b** You're introspective, preferring your own inner sanctum to the unpredictability of the outside world.
- **c** While at ease with yourself, you're not quite as comfortable with the world around you. You rely on certain environments to feel at peace.

7 POSITION WHEN RELAXING: How comfortable you are within yourself
- **a** You have an inner sense of calm and comfort – you're able to relax in your own skin.
- **b** You nurture an inner sense of vulnerability, which you guard closely.
- **c** While you use confidence as a front, you're not comfortable revealing the true you.

8 The three words you used to describe the animal indicate how you would like friends and loved ones to see you.

9 THE HOUSE: Your relationship with friends
- **a** You love and feel warmth towards many people, but in relationships you want more control, and need to be calling the shots. The lack of a fence indicates you're free and generous with affection, and new friends are welcome into your heart at any time.
- **b** You're comfortable with the buddies you've got and feel secure in your friendships with them. While you're warm and loving to your buddies, you don't throw your arms open to just any old person who happens to pass by.
- **c** You nurture relationships with a special few, and prefer privacy and intimacy over socialising. The buddies in your inner circle are very special to you and are held close to your heart.

10 THE SHAPE: How you act with your friends
- **a** Fitting in and pleasing your buds is important to you, and you're often caught in the middle during fights.
- **b** You're strong-willed, an individual and likely to be the leader of your pack.

11 THE PERSON: How you deal with problems
- **a** Faced with a problem, you'd rather ignore it and hope it blows over than address it directly.
- **b** You're good at dealing with dilemmas and usually approach them diplomatically.

12 THE ROUTE HOME: Your perspective on life
- **a** You live in the present, and savour different aspects of the world around you as they unfold. You're in no hurry to push forward into the next phase, and tend to flow in the direction that life is taking you.
- **b** You tire of situations easily and are often in a rush to bring on the next round of entertainment. Take care not to spend your life searching for more.